# BRINGING HOME
# THE HOUSING CRISIS

## Politics, Precarity and Domicide
## in Austerity London

Mel Nowicki

P

First published in Great Britain in 2023 by

Policy Press, an imprint of
Bristol University Press
University of Bristol
1–9 Old Park Hill
Bristol
BS2 8BB
UK
t: +44 (0)117 374 6645
e: bup-info@bristol.ac.uk

Details of international sales and distribution partners are available at
policy.bristoluniversitypress.co.uk

© Bristol University Press 2023

British Library Cataloguing in Publication Data
A catalogue record for this book is available from the British Library

ISBN 978-1-4473-6185-5 hardcover
ISBN 978-1-4473-6186-2 paperback
ISBN 978-1-4473-6187-9 ePub
ISBN 978-1-4473-6188-6 ePdf

Cover design: Robin Hawes
Front cover image: Stocksy/Alessandra Desole

For Sacha

# Contents

# Acknowledgements

First and foremost, I would like to thank all of my participants, and especially those who took the time to speak to me about their experiences of the bedroom tax, homelessness and the criminalisation of squatting. Your stories are the beating heart of this book, and I hope that I have done them justice.

Thanks to my editors Emily and Anna for their guidance and understanding throughout – particularly when I revealed that I was in my first trimester of pregnancy and therefore struggling to complete my draft on time! I would also like to thank my anonymous reviewer for their incredibly helpful and thoughtful comments on the first draft.

This book – and my career in general for that matter – would simply not exist without the unwavering support of my former PhD supervisor, my friend and mentor Katherine Brickell. Thank you so much for your guidance over the past nearly ten(!) years, it means so much.

Equally, I would like to thank my friend and colleague Ella Harris. Since we first met as wet-behind-the-ears PhD students, you have massively helped to shape my critical thinking, and been a most excellent partner in crime on our various research, conference and writing retreat adventures (it really does write itself when we work together). And special thanks to Katherine and Ella for being amazing colleagues on our research project with PLACE/Ladywell residents – Chapter 3 of this book belongs to you both as much as it does to me.

Finally, I would like to thank my mum Toni, my dad Vince, and my partner Jon for all their love and support throughout the writing of this book, my PhD, and my life in general. Very final thanks go to Sacha and Polly, who have not provided any support with the book writing, but are both extremely adorable.

# Introduction

In the early hours of the morning on Wednesday 14 June 2017, a fire broke out on the fourth floor of Grenfell Tower, a 24-storey high-rise residential block in North Kensington, London. Residents trapped in the tower were advised by the fire services to remain in their flats and wait for help, as the fire was assumed to be containable. However, as the night progressed it became clear this was not the case. The fire spread at high speed, trapping hundreds of residents in their homes as the flames tore through all 24 floors. It raged until the early hours of the following day, killing 72 people and destroying the homes of more than 200 households. The cause of the fire's rapid spread was quickly identified as the cladding that had been installed on the building's exterior a few years earlier by Kensington and Chelsea Council. The decision had been made to apply this particular cladding to Grenfell Tower in order to save around £300,000 in refurbishment costs. It emerged that the cladding, which has also been applied to hundreds of other residential (including my own former family home) and public buildings (including schools), was highly flammable and created cavities in the building, causing a chimney effect. This combination of factors is believed to have enabled the fire to sweep through the building at high speed.

Before the fire, Grenfell residents had warned of the dangers of the cladding, but their concerns were aggressively ignored. Indeed, it was revealed in the fire's aftermath that a local blogger expressing concern had been threatened with legal action by Kensington and Chelsea, who accused them of defamation and harassment (Roberts 2017). What was initially framed as a tragic accident was soon revealed to be the consequence of government (both local and national) negligence. At the time of writing, the Metropolitan Police are considering filing manslaughter, health and safety and fire safety charges against a number of companies and individuals – although Grenfell survivors remain deeply frustrated at the extraordinarily slow pace of these investigations (BBC 2021).

The day after the horrific event, then-Prime Minister Theresa May opened an inquiry into the fire – an inquiry that, at the time of writing, remains ongoing. So far, there have been multiple accusations of mismanagement, lack of investment and attempts to silence Grenfell survivors throughout the inquiry process. In his performance at the 2018 Brit Awards, grime artist Stormzy called out the government on their response with lyrics including: "Theresa May, where is the money for Grenfell? Just forgot about Grenfell, you criminals ... you should do some jail time, you should pay some damages, we should burn your house down and see if you can manage this" (Grenfell United, nd).

1

In the same year, Grenfell United, the main group representing survivors and the bereaved, initiated a successful campaign to force Theresa May to add further expertise to the controversial inquiry panel. As of August 2022, more than five years after the fire devastated hundreds of families and destroyed their homes, Grenfell residents continue to await rulings on the cladding's safety, the management of the tower, and central and local government responses to the disaster. In 2020, nine families still remained in temporary accommodation, one of these in a hotel. Even after a tragedy as high-profile as Grenfell, working-class lives and homes continue to be treated with contempt.

The Grenfell Tower fire is the amalgamation of the decades-long neglect of London's working-class residents. It is the horrific outcome of layer upon layer of policy and rhetoric that demarcates the worth of people's lives based on their housing tenure and socioeconomic background (Madden 2017). It is the unbearably tragic consequence of particular governance practices that deem the lives of lower-income and working-class people as lacking in economic and social value, and therefore unworthy of secure and liveable homes. Such neglect of Grenfell Tower and its residents reveals an approach to governance and housing that views the worth of life as hierarchical – that, to draw on the work of the political theorist Judith Butler, some lives are more grievable than others (Butler 2009). Those deemed to be on the lower rungs of society do not elicit much in the way of concern regarding access to safe and secure housing, as they are understood to have done little to deserve it. This is a form of domicide, meaning the intentional destruction of home (Porteous and Smith 2001), whereby the intentional neglect of safety measures in Grenfell Tower has ultimately contributed to the violent destruction of hundreds of homes, and the deaths of 72 people.

This book tells the story of how who does and does not deserve a home in the UK has been moulded and shaped by political rhetoric and housing policies. It is about how working-class and low-income people's access to secure and decent housing has been stripped away as a consequence. It is about how the concept of home has shifted, from a place that is fundamental to human security and happiness, to a financial product. And it is about how people have sought to challenge and resist this narrative. At the time of writing, we are emerging from a global pandemic that has brought into focus the importance of home. So many of us have spent unprecedented amounts of time where we live, our homes reconstructed as places of work, schooling and entertainment during government-mandated lockdowns. The pandemic has also writ large the deep inequalities embedded within housing markets – as home became ever-more central to our lives, it became apparent just how insecure and poor quality so many people's homes are. In short, now more than ever it has become clear just how much the right to home has been purposefully decimated over the past five decades, and what the long-term consequences are. This book is both an examination of that decimation, and a call to fight for a right to home for all. It does so through a focus on three case studies from the UK: the bedroom tax, the rise in family homelessness and temporary accommodation provision as its solution, and the criminalisation of squatting in a residential building. Central to the book are the experiences of those at the sharp end of these domicidal policies.

★ ★ ★

Around five years before the Grenfell fire, I heard two stories that got me thinking about the grossly unjust ways that policymaking penalises people based on where they call home, particularly in relation to their housing tenure (or lack thereof).

While visiting my aunt's for dinner one evening, I was shocked to hear that she was going to be hit by something called 'the bedroom tax'. She explained to me that she was suddenly going to lose a quarter of her housing benefit payment every month because she had two unoccupied rooms in her council flat (previously my grandmother's and lived in by many of my relatives over the years, including me). She was extremely anxious about this upcoming policy change, and had no idea where she was going to find the money to cover all of her rent. She had not worked for several years due to chronic physical and mental health conditions, and was understandably reluctant to either move from the flat she had lived in for almost all her life, or to have strangers renting out her rooms.

At a party later that week I bumped into an acquaintance from school. When I asked what he had been up to since then, he told me he had become involved with a socialist group, and had been squatting for a few years in south London. He recalled how he had enjoyed putting empty buildings back into use and saving money on rent while he studied. However, that had all come to an end for him, as the government had recently criminalised squatting in a residential building. He lamented that the law change had made it too difficult and too risky for him to continue squatting. He said he was lucky that he had friends and family he could stay with in London, and was able to remain in the city, but that friends he had squatted with had had little choice but to leave the capital, as rent was too expensive and their jobs too low-paying and precarious.

Both of these incidents struck me as appalling and illogical, particularly during a time that has been largely defined by housing crisis. This crisis is framed both in terms of lack of supply, and the unaffordability of the housing that does exist. The two policies felt paradoxical to me – why would the government introduce legislation that reduces people's housing options at a time when we are constantly told that housing availability is in crisis? I wanted to explore the issue more, and decided to pursue a research degree examining the impacts of these two policies that had so negatively affected people around me. From this, I hoped to gain an understanding of how and why these policies had been brought into being in the first place, what the impacts have been on the people they target, if and how people were challenging and resisting them, and to what extent these challenges had been successful. Although the bedroom tax and criminalisation of squatting affect England and Wales[1] as a whole, I decided to focus my research on London (for reasons explained later in this chapter).

As my doctoral degree progressed, I also began to learn more about related housing injustices running rampant through the city. In 2016, myself, my supervisor Katherine Brickell and fellow PhD student Ella Harris heard about PLACE/Ladywell, a so-called 'pop-up' social housing scheme being developed in the borough of Lewisham. As my research focused on social housing, and Ella's on pop-up culture, we decided to learn more about the scheme. Our resulting research findings, which make up the majority of Chapter 3 of this book, opened the door to a whole new set of housing injustices – namely, the exponential rise of families being evicted from the private rented sector, becoming homeless, and forced to live in 'temporary' accommodation, often for years. In this context, PLACE/Ladywell represents a purported solution to these issues through a growing focus on the construction of purpose-built temporary accommodation. This struck me as being tied up in the same issues I was exploring in relation to the bedroom tax and the criminalisation of squatting. It is true that, unlike the other two policies, the development of relatively high-quality temporary accommodation such as PLACE/Ladywell can be seen as a positive development for people in housing crisis. However, as I argue in more detail in Chapter 3, the focus on temporary accommodation as a solution merely exemplifies just how normalised precarious and insecure housing has become – especially for working-class and low-income people.

All three policies can be traced back to the construction of narratives that deem some people as deserving of home, and others as undeserving. Throughout my research, it was clear that this ran very much along lines of class and housing tenure, with middle-class homeowners celebrated as the makers of ideal homes, and working-class, low-income non-homeowners derided as the opposite. This appeared to be especially true in relation to social tenants, single parent families in need of welfare support, and squatters – all in varying ways framed as scroungers, reaping the benefits of others' hard work. These linkages felt increasingly important to explore together.

During this time I also encountered the term 'domicide'. First coined by two Canadian geographers, J. Douglas Porteous and Sandra E. Smith in their seminal 2001 book, domicide refers to the intentional destruction

4

of home, including but not exclusive to, the destruction of housing. In their book, Porteous and Smith recount the varying scales where domicide occurs, dividing their examples into 'extreme' and 'everyday' categories. Extreme domicide refers to instances where entire communities are displaced, for example through war and the colonial theft of Indigenous lands. Everyday domicide refers to smaller-scale instances of home loss, for example the purposeful destruction of housing to make way for damming projects. As I read more about the concept of home, and its destruction, I began to think about how legislation like the bedroom tax, temporary accommodation policies and the criminalisation of squatting might, too, be considered domicide, albeit in a different way to Porteous and Smith's definitions. There was the obvious similarity with their examples, particularly in that all three policies utilise, to varying degrees, forced eviction – the intentional removal of people from the places they call home. But I also began to think about how domicide was functioning in another, more subtle way. These policies were not just trying to remove people from their dwellings, they were also working to discredit particular groups' right to have any form of home in the first place. This struck me as perhaps even more insipid and dangerous than the forced eviction itself, as it bore with it the construction by national government, who supposedly exist to protect and serve its citizens and residents, of a system that claims not everyone is entitled to a decent and secure home. I have termed this somewhat less tangible, but no less powerful, process 'socio-symbolic domicide' (more on this in Chapter 1) (Nowicki 2014).

This book focuses on the impact of the bedroom tax (officially titled the 'removal of the spare room subsidy'), rising family homelessness and temporary accommodation-oriented policy solutions, and the criminalisation of squatting (section 144 of the Legal Aid, Sentencing and Punishment of Offenders Act 2012).[2] However, the stories told and issues raised throughout also speak to a wider set of malign governance practices that denounce working-class and low-income people – in particular those who are not seen to subscribe to aspirations of homeownership – as worthless. Earlier in this introduction I gave an account of the Grenfell Tower fire as it is a highly visceral, tragic and enraging example of the consequences of multiple layers of neglect, dismissal and the denigration of some of London's most vulnerable communities. Through this book, I hope to contribute to a call for accountability and a demand for justice for the generations of Londoners who have been discounted by governance practices that denounce their very rights to home, in part on the basis of their class and housing tenure. While class-based discrimination is far from the only way in which inequality is built into housing systems, and intersects with many other forms of discrimination, it nonetheless remains central to the stories told in this book. The UK has long had a special obsession with class, and home, like so many other important spaces in our lives, has been shaped through a classed lens. Indeed, the very nature of the so-called housing crisis of the past decade or so has largely been attributed to an overemphasis on welfare and the over-subsidisation of an irresponsible working class.

Unaffordability and housing insecurity in London is regularly portrayed as a crisis borne out of the former UK Labour government's economic irresponsibility. This has somehow become the presiding narrative, despite the very global nature of the 2008 financial crash and its aftermath. We have now long been told that more housing is not being built because no one can afford to build it; that affordable housing is not financially viable. That this crisis is a moment in time, and that once we have balanced the national books through a programme of years-long austerity measures housebuilding levels and affordability will improve. However, as Madden and Marcuse (2016) note, to continue to call current housing conditions one of crisis is inherently misleading. What we are seeing take place in London, and countless other cities across the globe, is not an acute housing crisis, a passing moment in time. Rather, it is the long-term normalisation of housing precarity for select groups of people, for the benefit of wealthy elites. As they note:

> Housing crisis is a predictable, consistent outcome of a basic characteristic of capitalist spatial development: housing is not distributed for the purposes of dwelling for all; it is produced and distributed as a commodity to enrich the few. Housing crisis is not a result of the system breaking down but of the system working as it intended. (Madden and Marcuse 2016: 10)

This book is in part a consolidation of this point. I argue that the bedroom tax, the prioritisation of temporary accommodation policies, and the criminalisation of squatting are not the necessary consequences of a housing crisis. Rather, they are deliberate attempts to undermine, and ultimately eradicate, the legitimacy of forms of home that are not in keeping with neoliberal ideals of housing as primarily a source of profit and financial investment. In short, this is a targeted housing crisis that dismantles working-class and low-income people's very right to a home.

This book explores issues around the normalisation of precarious housing through examining how political rhetoric, and the policies that follow on from that rhetoric, actively and purposefully dismantle rights to home for those who are already some of the city's most vulnerable and precariously housed. The concept of home is central to my analysis, and I argue that we cannot fully assess the causes and impacts of, and potential solutions to, the precaritisation of housing and the demonisation of low-income people without an acknowledgement of the central role of home. Home is an integral site through which our personal and collective identities are constructed, a site of comfort, of alienation, of safety, of fear (Blunt and Dowling 2006). My exploration of the three case studies in this book provides an account of what happens when rights to home are intentionally destroyed.

## Distinguishing housing from home

Although clearly interconnected terms, it is important to note that *home* should not be conflated with *housing*. Housing refers to the material dwelling, while home relates to a much more expansive, more emotive set of ideas – although housing is of course often part of how we define home. Home can vary drastically in scale, from dwelling, to nation, and beyond. It can refer to the material (for example, a dwelling), or a broader set of feelings, such as security and familiarity. Although widely understood as an inherently positive space, the home can equally be imbued with precarity, violence and loss, as feminist geographers such as Katherine Brickell have explored in their work on domestic violence and relationship breakdown (Brickell 2012a, 2012b).

Although this book is concerned with the impact of particular housing policies, what is most profound and far-reaching about them are their implications for people's rights to *home*. As my research attests, the destruction and denial of one's home and, perhaps most importantly of all, a sociopolitical climate that deems particular people not deserving of home at all, moves beyond issues connected to housing alone. This book does not solely tell the story of a perceived crisis in the housing system, but also of a social crisis, in which those deemed to be undesirable and unproductive are stripped of the basic right to home – to feel secure, to feel safe, to feel that they belong. How the home is both experienced by individuals and constructed in policy rhetoric has wide-reaching political implications, determining human value through the idealisation of some homes and the dismissal of others. In short, home matters, and should be taken seriously as a concept.

While rights to the city have long been theorised in the social sciences (Mitchell 2003; Lefebvre 2014), and formed the basis of much urban activism, less attention has been paid to legal, social and cultural rights to home and home life. Just as our ability to shape the urban landscape is fundamental to our experience of and wellbeing within the city, so too is our ability to construct, secure and maintain a home integral to our ability to live fulfilling lives. This book is a recounting of what happens when the home becomes a perpetual site of precarity for those whose lives are already precarious. Beyond this, it also considers the wider impact of denouncing swathes of people as undeserving of a secure home.

## Legitimising domicide: enter the 'age of austerity'

The last decade or so in the West has been largely defined by austerity politics, although this was superseded somewhat by the arrival of COVID-19 in early 2020. However, even before this shift in era nomenclature had occurred, politicians such as then-UK Prime Minister Theresa May were declaring in 2018 that austerity was 'over'. And yet, while the terminology of austerity was somewhat knocked out of mainstream consciousness in the late 2010s, the effects of austerity politics continue to wreak havoc on many aspects of people's lives, including their homes. This is most recently apparent in what has been termed in 2022 the 'cost of living crisis'. This newest iteration of crisis is characterised by rising levels of inflation and an acceleration in the cost of fuel, food and other everyday items. The UK government has been careful to frame the new wave of precarity and decreasing quality of life as a consequence of uncontrollable external factors such as the pandemic and 2022 Russian invasion of Ukraine. The term austerity has so far remained relatively absent from political rhetoric regarding this latest crisis. However, its legacy is evident in the continued growing unaffordability of housing, rising rates of precarious employment and a welfare system – including the National Health Service that saved so many lives during the pandemic – whose funding has been squeezed year on year. But how exactly did the global financial crash and its economic and political aftermath lead to the enactment of domicidal policies such as the bedroom tax, the rise of temporary accommodation and the criminalisation of squatting? In short, the crash established the groundwork for reworking narratives regarding who does – and crucially, does not – deserve the right to home.

The Labour Party were largely seen to have lost the 2010 general election on the basis that they had been responsible for the recession that followed the 2008 crash. It was therefore through a return to rhetoric made famous by Margaret Thatcher that emphasised 'balancing the books' and reducing the nation's deficit that the Conservative Party were able to return to power. The new leadership, under David Cameron, came with warnings that in order to right the financial wrongs committed by Labour, economic austerity would inevitably have to be implemented until the economy improved. In a 2009 speech prior to his election as prime minister, Cameron referred to a future Conservative government providing: "a whole new, never-been-done-before approach to the way this country is run. Why? Because the world has completely changed. In this new world comes the reckoning for Labour's economic incompetence. The age of irresponsibility is giving way to the age of austerity" (Cameron 2009).

The financial crisis was ideologically reworked by the Conservative Party and other right-wing institutions from an issue of global economics to one of Labour's national overspend on welfare (Clarke and Newman 2012;

Bramall 2013). The 'age of austerity' pronounced by Cameron in 2009 framed the recession as a consequence of, as John Clarke and Janet Newman have put it, 'the unwieldy and expensive welfare state and public sector, rather than the high risk strategies of banks, as the root cause of the crisis' (Clarke and Newman 2012: 300). Financial recession, therefore, enabled Cameron's government to present those in receipt of welfare as both part of the root cause of the crisis, and a threat to future financial stability. Low-income people were increasingly narrativised as having a negative impact on the livelihoods of morally upstanding, financially responsible property owners. This was in large part achieved by framing welfare expenditure as an unnecessary burden on the taxpayer (Slater 2016a). John Clarke and Janet Newman attribute this to what they term 'magical thinking' – the idea that if something is asserted in the public sphere often enough, it will take on a sense of 'truth' (Clarke and Newman 2012). As the geographer Tom Slater notes, 'the Tories in Britain have transformed the 2007–2008 crisis of capitalism into a crisis of the welfare state' (2016a: 26). Such depictions of the financial crisis being caused by a bloated welfare state and 'soft' legal system (re)enabled a set of logics that reasserted and extended neoliberalism[3] as foundational to British politics (Hodkinson and Robbins 2013). This re-commitment to the neoliberal cause, therefore, set the scene for a regime of welfare cuts, including the bedroom tax and vast reductions in local authority housebuilding, as necessary, pragmatic and morally just solutions to the 'age of irresponsibility'.

Austerity rhetoric, therefore, constructs social and economic precarity as inevitable. Austerity is understood as the only process by which to reduce state spending on welfare, and thus stabilise the economy. This normalisation of austerity, in turn, justifies the instalment of further precarity into the lives of working-class and low-income people, framed as an act of restoring both the nation's economy and social morality. By reinstating 'fairness' into the welfare system and purportedly protecting particular groups, such as homeowners, who are deemed morally and economically admirable, austerity was subsumed into the everyday in the post-recession landscape. Austerity, then, repackages the precaritisation of working-class and low-income people as both a necessary and moral framework for establishing a fairer society. Through an in-depth exploration of the bedroom tax, rise of temporary accommodation policies, and the criminalisation of squatting, this book seeks to better understand this shifting rhetoric and what it means for the lives of those most acutely affected. Investigating the ways in which austerity has normalised precarity has become ever-more crucial as we – at the time of writing – enter the latest era of so-called crisis. It is only through understanding how the rights of large swathes of people have been decimated that we might learn how to undo some of these now hard-wired narratives regarding who is and is not deserving of home, of security, of belonging.

## Project research methods

Methodologically, this book centres on sharing the experiences of people living on the front lines of housing precarity in London. The stories, findings and ideas that make up *Bringing Home the Housing Crisis* were collated using three methods. First, and primarily, interviews were conducted with a wide range of participants[4] – social tenants impacted by the bedroom tax, families living in temporary accommodation, squatters, housing charity and association employees, housing activists, architects and MPs. Participants were recruited either through direct contact (email, messaging on social media, and in some cases good old-fashioned door-knocking), or through 'snowballing'.[5] Interview locations varied, from people's homes, to offices and cafes (and in one memorable instance, a graveyard). This was the predominant method of the project, as sharing the stories of those impacted by the policies lies at the heart of the book.

At times I found it difficult to reconcile the fact that I was asking relative strangers to share with me potentially traumatic life events, delving into deeply intimate subject areas around financial and emotional struggles, and asking them to reflect on how they felt they were perceived in the public imagination. As Sara Smith (2014: 142) asks, 'how can the intimacies of fieldwork be translated to the written page without indulgence?'. How could I tell these at times traumatic stories in the most appropriate and effective way? These concerns have followed me throughout the research process, as well they should. And yet it is these intimate conversations, these enraging and upsetting encounters, that perhaps need to be told the most. I hope that the realities of domicide will contribute to the ever-growing body of research and activism that calls out housing, urban and class injustice, and demands change. With this in mind, I have done my utmost to approach the research material with respect, and with the understanding that I have a social responsibility to engage others in what I have learned.

While listening to and collating people's experiences was central, I also found other, complementary methods useful in expanding discussion and ideas. A second method involved analysing a range of political speeches, policy reports and media articles using critical discourse analysis. Critical discourse analysis is a research method that deconstructs the ways in which political and social structures are invoked and implemented. Through examining the documents that establish and cement these structures, critical discourse analysis seeks to reveal 'buried ideology' through analysing and critiquing the relationship between power structures, language and knowledge discourse (Machin and Mayr 2012). Through analysis of political speeches in particular, a stronger understanding of socio-symbolic domicide as a political tool was better established.

Third, I engaged in what has been termed 'political ethnography' – meaning a holistic engagement with a particular political issue (Forrest 2017). This can include, but is not limited to, involvement in activist groups, attendance at protest events, or spending time with people belonging to political subcultures. As the project progressed, my understanding of the three case study policies and the broader housing crisis became shaped not only through the interviews I conducted and the speeches I analysed, but also through my own engagement with housing activism. I gave talks at various grassroots housing activism conferences and discussion days, attended rallies and protests, and spent time in squatted social centres and other activist spaces. Along with interviews and critical discourse analysis, a political ethnography approach centres on ascertaining the varying power relations and dynamics that both construct unequal sociopolitical landscapes, and explores the ways in which such dynamics are tested and challenged (Schatz 2009; Forrest 2017). Together, these methods provided me with a wide-ranging oversight into the establishment and impact of, and resistance to, domicidal housing policies.

## Research location: focusing on London

Although the three key case studies of this book are applicable across the entirety of the UK in the case of temporary accommodation policies, and across England and Wales in the case of the bedroom tax and criminalisation of squatting, I chose to focus on London as the project's research site. There are two main reasons behind this decision. First, although the housing crisis is by no means a London-specific problem, it is particularly extreme in the capital (Dorling 2014). Historically low housebuilding and an ever-dwindling social housing stock is compounded by drastically soaring house prices. By 2016, house prices had risen by 39 per cent since pre-recession levels, rising by 13.9 per cent from March 2015–16 alone (Government Land Registry 2016). Although the rise in the capital's house prices has slowed in recent years due to both Brexit and the coronavirus pandemic, the average house price in London was £530,000 as of April 2022, almost double the average price in the UK as a whole (Office for National Statistics 2022). The growing unaffordability of the capital, and the ever-expanding inequality between rich and poor – geographer and inequality expert Danny Dorling has cited London as the most unequal city in the developed world – situates the city as an integral research site in understanding the effect of punitive housing policies on working-class and low-income people (Dorling 2011).

While the bedroom tax has affected households across England and Wales, a large proportion are situated in London. Alongside this, the high cost of rent in London means that social tenants in receipt of housing benefit lose far more in rent support in the capital than in any other part of the country (Department for Work and Pensions 2015). This inevitably leaves them at greater risk of arrears, indebtedness and eviction. This, coupled with growing concerns around the increasing displacement of social tenants in London through so-called regeneration schemes that regularly replace social housing with high-cost private properties (see for example Campkin 2013; Watt 2013; Lees 2014), makes London an important site for understanding the destruction of social tenants' rights to home. Equally, while rising rates of family homelessness and reliance on temporary accommodation as a solution are far from exclusive to London, it is an especially acute problem there. According to the Trust for London, every one of London's 32 boroughs has a higher proportion of households living in temporary accommodation than the England average (Trust for London 2021). This is hardly surprising considering the extortionate costs of living in the capital.

Finally, London was a logical choice of location to explore the criminalisation of squatting and its impact. This is due to the fact that the UK squatting scene is largely concentrated in London. It must be noted here that reliable data on squatter numbers and their whereabouts is difficult to obtain due to the hidden and transient nature of the practice (particularly in the post-section 144 landscape). In 2010 the government estimated that there were 20,000 squatters in the country, and no official estimations have been made since (Ministry of Justice 2011). However, prior to beginning my research I had several conversations with existing contacts connected to squatting both locally and nationally. All informed me that the dominant squatting scene was in London. Taking advice from those engaged in squatting, along with secondary knowledge of London as a longstanding hub of squatting culture since the post-war era, reaffirmed my decision to base the research project in the capital (Platt 1999; Finchett-Maddock 2014; Reeve 2015).

However, while the case studies in this book take a focused look at London, the issues raised and struggles faced reach far beyond the UK capital. The stories shared across the next five chapters may be specific in one sense, but in another they are universal. They are the stories of marginalised people who have been constructed as undeserving of home, a process that in turn legitimises further destructive policymaking and legislation. This unfortunately is a globally recognised struggle. While the domicide being enacted may take different forms, the consequences are often the same – poverty, displacement, loss of identity, poor mental health. Time and again already precarious people are made more so for the purposes of furthering elitism and inequality of resources. This may be a story about London, but it is one that many outside of the city will recognise.

## Overview of the book

The remainder of the book is divided into five main chapters and a conclusion. Chapter 1 outlines the concept of home and its political importance. I begin by discussing how the home was long considered a politics-free space – diametrically opposed to the 'public' sphere. I draw on the work of feminist theorists such as Cynthia Enloe, Mona Domosh and Katherine Brickell, who argue that the home is in fact a highly political site. For example, home is where we are taught to adopt assumed gender roles, and protecting the 'homeland' is a common and powerful rhetoric used by politicians to instil anti-immigration sentiment.

The chapter then turns to the interrelated concepts of stigma, precarity and domicide – the intentional destruction of home. I go on to outline how I have extended the term to consider more subtle, narrative-led, forms of home destruction – a process I term 'socio-symbolic domicide'. I iterate how this is central to the book's argument – that the concept of home is manipulated and moralised in politics and the media across a range of global contexts, creating narratives of people who are 'deserving' and 'undeserving' of it.

Finally, the chapter goes on to trace this moralisation in the UK context specifically through housing tenure. I focus on Margaret Thatcher's premiership and the so-called 'neoliberal turn' of the 1970s and 80s. Through a discussion of Thatcher's housing policy, I highlight how the concept of home was re-narrativised in this period, with a focus on private homeownership as the key to a successful home life, and therefore a successful nation. I go on to examine how this fundamental ideological shift continued through subsequent New Labour governments. The chapter then considers the ways in which this new vision of 'home' was utilised by the 2010–15 Conservative/Liberal Democrat Coalition government in the context of austerity. Finally, the chapter concludes by considering the continued influence of politics that moralises the home, with a focus on the 2016 Brexit referendum and ongoing coronavirus pandemic.

Chapter 2 turns to the book's first case study, the bedroom tax. In order to contextualise the policy, I begin by providing a brief history of social tenancy in the UK. The chapter then outlines the introduction of, and impetus behind, the 2012 Welfare Reform Act, which includes the bedroom tax. I go on to explore initial media and political responses to the policy, before turning focus to the financial and emotional hardships experienced by social tenants affected. The remainder of the chapter traces the multitude of ways in which social tenants are left struggling to remain in their homes, as well as assert their right to home in the first place. I begin by exploring how fear of forced eviction contributes to loss of autonomy and security regarding home. The chapter goes on to explore the impact of the bedroom tax on mental health and wellbeing. I then change tack slightly to consider how the Coalition government simultaneously introduced a range of welfare schemes designed to support middle-class people looking to buy their first property. I argue this is key in understanding just how much rights to home and state support differ along class lines. The chapter concludes by considering the ways in which social tenants internalise domicide, understanding themselves as undeserving of home in what is arguably one of the most pernicious impacts of the bedroom tax.

Chapter 3 shifts focus to the private rented sector, and in particular the growing policy emphasis on temporary accommodation provision. I begin by highlighting the increased prevalence of private renting. I look at the ways in which precarity is built into the private sector through laws that enable no-fault evictions at short notice. The chapter highlights how this is a perfect storm in an era of austerity, where rising rents coupled with falling incomes have increased evictions from the private rented sector and subsequent homelessness. I explore the particular impact this has had on families, recounting London families' experiences of eviction and homelessness, often resulting in weeks, months, or even years spent living in poor-quality and unsuitable temporary accommodation. The second part of the chapter turns to look at local and national approaches to addressing these issues through purpose-built temporary accommodation. I do so through an in-depth discussion of PLACE/Ladywell, a so-called 'pop-up' temporary accommodation scheme in south London. I outline its successes, as well as concerns regarding the long-term benefits of the scheme. The chapter concludes with a discussion of increasingly pernicious forms of temporary accommodation provision. I caution against an overemphasis on the provision of temporary accommodation, even those that are high quality, at the expense of building permanent social housing. I argue that such focus on purpose-built temporary accommodation, even if well-intentioned, ultimately further normalises working-class and low-income people as undeserving of secure homes.

Chapter 4 explores the impact of the criminalisation of squatting in England and Wales – via section 144 of the Legal Aid, Sentencing and Punishment of Offenders Act 2012 – on London's squatting community. I begin by providing a brief overview of squatting culture in London since the mid-twentieth century, the fluctuating levels of suspicion and stigma regarding the practice, and how anti-squatting sentiment became cemented as emphasis on the importance of property ownership grew. The chapter then outlines the events that led to the introduction of section 144. I go on to explore squatters' experiences of the increasing regularity of forced eviction. The next part of the chapter examines the impact on squatters' mental health and wellbeing of being forced to live in larger, less stable communities. I then look at the ways in which squatters are increasingly forced to justify their existence, for example as political and environmental activists, and the ways in which this further detaches the practice of squatting from one of homemaking. The chapter concludes by exploring the phenomenon of 'property guardianships' – firms that rent out empty properties on behalf of landlords to 'guardians' to protect buildings from squatters, while at the same time appropriating squatter lifestyles. I argue that this practice signifies the ways in which squatting is simultaneously being erased and resurrected in a profitable capitalist format.

Chapter 5 turns to consider the ways in which political attacks on home over the past decade have been resisted and challenged in a variety of ways. The chapter begins by exploring how activists have used legal frameworks to fight back against domicidal housing policies, for example social tenants taking the government to court over the discriminatory nature of the bedroom tax. The chapter then turns to more micro-scale 'everyday' forms of resistance, focusing on the example of a squatter crew disguising their squat as a hipster shop in order to hide in plain sight in gentrified London. I go on to examine the role of language use in resistance, particularly shifting terminology from 'squatting' to 'occupation' in order to enable a range of direct action responses to domicide. Finally, the chapter considers so-called 'banal' forms of resistance, exploring the ways in which homeless families work to reassert their dignity and right to home through material objects.

The book concludes by bringing together the arguments of the five main chapters to call for greater attention to be paid to home as an integral human right. It outlines the policy contributions of the book – highlighting the need to repeal the bedroom tax, section 144 and regulate the private rented sector. Following this, the conclusion reiterates the conceptual relevance of the book, in both extending the concept of domicide to consider the ways in which the home can be decimated beyond the destruction of or removal from the dwelling, and in better connecting critical geographies of home and housing studies. The chapter goes on to provide a brief update of the political landscape since the research for this book was conducted, before highlighting how the so-called 'housing crisis' has become a normalised condition in London, the UK and beyond. I end by asserting that it is only through rethinking what we mean by 'home', and how this connects to housing policy, that London can become a place that all, regardless of class, status or tenure, have a right to call home.

# 1

# The politicisation of home

## 'Moving past the front stoop': critical geographies of home

All that is discussed and analysed throughout this book can be traced back to one word: home. *Bringing Home the Housing Crisis* is fundamentally about our relationship with home, who is portrayed as deserving of it, what happens when it is taken away from us, and how we fight back in order to regain it. Although now a growing sub-discipline, particularly within human geography, it has only been in the past two decades or so that the key social and political roles of the home have begun to be taken seriously by academics.

Much academic work has focused on the home in relation to belonging, comfort and material culture (Manzo 2003). There exists an extensive and ever-growing body of literature that explores the nature and nuances of people's emotional relationships to the homespace (see for example, Miller 2001; 2008; Blunt and Varley 2004; Burrell 2014). This includes literature focusing on senses of place, place attachment and place identity. Within this work, the home is usually understood as an intrinsically positive site. This was particularly true up until the mid-1990s, with scholars such as the sociologist Peter Saunders for example insisting that there were no gendered divisions or tensions within the confines of the home. Based on a household survey (whose participants were exclusively middle-class) he asserted that there are no differences in the way men and women view meanings of home (Saunders 1988). The sociologist Peter Somerville, in a similar vein, produced a supposedly objective set of signifiers of home in the early 1990s, consisting of: shelter, hearth, heart, privacy, roots, abode and paradise (Somerville 1992).

Such attempts to quantify home and its meanings hugely oversimplified the complex relationship people have with it, in particular overlooking negative aspects of home – for example, as a site of women's oppression or domestic violence (Blunt and Dowling 2006). Such unchallenged associations of home equalling comfort led feminist scholars to critique this somewhat benign approach (Sibley 1995). Over the last three decades, feminist geographers in particular have spearheaded a more critical approach to the concept of home, urging us at the end of the twentieth century to 'move past the front stoop' (Domosh 1998: 276) to consider the home as an important political and social site. Following a seminal conference on 'Geographies of Home' at University College London in 2000, and a subsequent 2004 special edition of the journal *cultural geographies*, home began for the first time to be taken seriously as a vital subject in understanding the politics of the everyday (Blunt and Varley 2004; Blunt 2005). Once seen as mundane and irrelevant, the banality of everyday practices within the home, such as cooking, decorating and other forms of domestic work, were considered in a new light (Blunt and Varley 2004; Enloe 2011). Cultural and feminist geographers such as Mark Llewellyn (2004) and Janet Floyd (2004), for example, considered the domestic kitchen as both a site of the reinforcement of gender roles, and as a potential site for the (re)negotiation of gender, class and national identities through the breaking down of these traditional roles. Geographies of home as a critical academic field in its own right was concretised by the publication of Alison Blunt and Robyn Dowling's book *Home* (2006). Here, home was considered across truly multi-scalar sites, its location, meaning and imaginings stretching from the dwelling, to the neighbourhood, to the nation. Through these multiple scales and contexts, Blunt and Dowling encouraged the consideration of home beyond traditional essentialist and humanistic representations of it as sacred, apolitical space. Moving beyond such binary conceptualisations of the home (see Relph 1976; Csikzentmihalyi and Rochberg-Halton 1981; Dovey 1985; Terkenli 1995), geographers in particular have, in recent years, argued that the home is in fact an intrinsically political site, not only passively affected and shaped by governance and social and political shifts, but one that itself actively impacts wider politics (Brickell 2012a). For example, the home has been increasingly understood as a site through which gender, class and racial identities and performativities are constructed, enacted, reinforced and resisted (Blunt and Dowling 2006; Brickell 2012b).

The pertinence of home as a national governance strategy has also become increasingly acknowledged across the social sciences. Professor of politics William Walters coined the term 'domopolitics' to express this intrinsic relationship between the home and governance practices (Walters 2004). As he notes, domopolitics articulates modes of governance and power that imply 'a reconfiguration of the relationship between citizenship, state, and territory. At its heart is a fateful conjunction of home, land and security' (2004: 241). Walters distinguishes domopolitics from previous articulations of political governance economy, traditionally allegorised as being akin to the governance of a household. Governance of the state as *home* rather than *household*, Walters argues, attends to the rationale of neoliberal governance practices beyond solely improving the economic efficiency and output of citizens. Rather, domopolitics constructs a relationship between citizens and the nation through an emphasis on social and cultural, as well as economic, prisms. This ensures the securitisation of the nation-state through a politics of affectation that binds the nation to traditional depictions of home as hearth, as a site of safety that both protects and is in need of protection (Walters 2004; Hynek 2012). An integral function of domopolitics, then, is how it juxtaposes affectations of the homely nation-state against the external threats of the 'outside world', a particular configuration of 'us vs. them' depictions of nationhood and security that implicitly mobilises, generates and legitimises fear of those deemed external to the safe confinement of the homespace (Walters 2004; Darling 2011; Hynek 2012). Walters examines this binary through the example of the USA's Department of Homeland Security as an explicit framing of the nation-state as a homespace in need of protection from unhomely external forces. In the UK context, politics academic Joe Turner applied the concept of domopolitics to his research examining the infamous 2011 eviction of Irish Traveller communities from the Dale Farm site in Essex (Turner 2016). He argues that the eviction was justified through an ongoing political framing of home and domesticity that outcasts the homemaking practices of Travellers as 'failing' domestic norms, and thus failing as citizens (Turner 2016). This mobilisation of domestic space to differentiate between 'successful' and 'failed' people lies very much at the heart of this book, as will be explored in greater detail across the four case study chapters.

## Bringing housing studies home

The home has gained traction among social scientists in recent decades as a crucial concept in understanding the interconnections between the political and the everyday (Brickell 2012a). This growing body of research highlights that understandings of home must, in part, move beyond dwellings alone. Clearly, home can, and should, be considered in a wide array of contexts and across geographical scales.

Having said this, housing of course remains integral to critical studies of home. While the two should not be conflated with one another, they are nonetheless clearly interconnected in many ways (Smith 2008; Atkinson and Jacobs 2016). For most people, housing forms a focal point for homemaking practices and establishing senses of belonging and self. Equally, housing can be a key contributor in instances of home *un*making, for example through the demolition of, or forced eviction from, housing (Brickell et al 2017) – more on which later in the chapter. Housing, then, is often at the centre of our understandings of home, and at the centre of policies and practices that seek to destroy our sense of home.

However, despite these clear connections, for many years housing studies scholarship tended to overlook the concept of home (Atkinson and Jacobs 2016). Home was largely dismissed as a 'soft' term lacking quantifiable meaning. However, housing scholars such as Susan Smith and David Morley sought to redress this lack of dialogue between housing studies and conceptualisations of home (Morley 2003; Smith 2008). For example, in an account of the relationship between homeownership, the marketisation of housing and meanings of home, Smith explores the ways in which the financialisation of housing interacts with the micropolitics of home. She examines homeowners' understanding of, and behaviour in relation to, their property as increasingly central in their and their families' future security. In short, that housing as a financial asset is entangled with homeowners' sense of home. This is particularly pertinent in an era in which housing is increasingly marketed as primarily a space of financial consumption and profitability (Aalbers 2016). Smith argues that this financialisation of housing does not detract from its importance as a site of home construction. Rather, the two are complexly enmeshed with one another, as 'financial services and housing economics thread savings, spending, and debt through the fabric of housing and home' (Smith 2008: 530).

The current and future implications of the financialisation of housing has established itself rightly as a crucial area of study, highlighting the structural inequalities embedded within housing markets (Rolnik 2003; Aalbers 2016; Fernandez and Aalbers 2016). The term 'housing crisis' is continually bandied across academia, political discourse, the media and in the public lexicon more broadly as a crisis of economy. However, little mention is made of the ways in which the relationship between market forces, housing and national and international economies impact people's home lives, their senses of home, their loss of home. As I highlighted in the introduction, the housing crisis is far from merely the consequence of financial recession. It is the consequence of a decades-long ideological project that has sought to sever understandings of housing from the human need for home, repackaging housing as a source of financial profiteering over and above a fundamental site of human identity construction (Madden and Marcuse 2016). Now, more than ever, housing and home scholars need to forge better dialogue in order to challenge this now-normative understanding of home. My hope for this book is that it will contribute to extending such dialogue.

## Destroying the home: domicide and home unmaking

In this book, I am especially concerned with conceptualisations of the home in circumstances where the homespace comes under threat from housing policy and law-making. Therefore, much of the discussion within these pages of the bedroom tax, the rise of temporary accommodation policies, and the criminalisation of squatting looks to understand what the consequences are when home is purposefully dismantled – when it is *intentionally destroyed*. The home lives of low-income, working-class and other politically precarious people have, particularly over the last decade or so, been shaped by their destruction, and the subsequent adjustments to everyday life that have to be made in the face of reduced rights to home. In particular, I have found the term 'domicide' crucial in determining both how and why the policy and legislative decisions central to this book destroy homelives, and how new approaches to homemaking are constructed in the face of these aggressive governance practices.

## Domicide

Domicide, the intentional destruction of home, is a concept first coined by Canadian geographers J. Douglas Porteous and Sandra E. Smith in their 2001 book *Domicide: The Global Destruction of Home*. *Domicide* is a detailed portrayal of 'the deliberate destruction of home by human agency in the pursuit of specific goals, which causes suffering to the victims' (Porteous and Smith 2001: 12). Using the categories 'extreme' and 'everyday', the authors cite a wide range of examples across the globe of domicide and its impact. *Extreme* domicide focuses on the destruction of the homespace on a grand scale through three key mediums: war (for example, US carpet bombing in the 1960s and 70s intentionally targeting villages in Vietnam, Laos and Cambodia); 'colonial geopiracy' (for instance, the forced removal of Indigenous people from their ancestral homelands by white settlers); and resettlement projects (such as ethnic segregation in apartheid-era South Africa). Porteous and Smith then consider the impact of so-called *everyday* forms of domicide, which they define as such: 'unlike extreme domicide, the everyday variety comes about because of the normal, mundane operations of the world's political economy' (2001: 106). Focusing on an example of dam construction in British Columbia, their typology of everyday domicide emphasises its localised scale, whereby homes, neighbourhoods and smaller settlements are demolished to make way for political and/or corporate interests.

Porteous and Smith's work provides a significant contribution to critical conceptualisations of home, highlighting the multifaceted ways in which homes can be deliberately destroyed under the auspices of ideology and political pragmatism. However, their discussions of domicide tend to retain a focus on the destruction of, or displacement from, the physical dwelling. While highlighting the trauma of these particular manifestations of domicide is undoubtedly extremely important in understanding the implications of home destruction, to limit conceptualisations of domicide solely to the materiality of the house potentially renders invisible its subtler social, cultural and political consequences. I argue that it is important to extend domicide further, to consider the home and its destruction beyond the physical alone and explore what I term its *socio-symbolic* forms as well (Nowicki 2014). As Alison Blunt and Robyn Dowling note: 'home ... is a *place*, a site in which we live. But, more than this, home is also an idea and an imaginary that is imbued with feelings' (2006: 2). The home does not consist solely of bricks and mortar, and can be dismantled and destroyed in a variety of forms. As Gearóid Ó Tuathail and Carl Dahlman note in relation to their work on post-genocide Bosnia, domicide is 'the erasure of the spatiality of home not necessarily the destruction of property' (2006: 245). In their tracing of the Bosnian post-war landscape, Ó Tuathail and Dahlman consider the ways in which Bosnian people's sense of home was violently erased. More than two million people were displaced by the war, losing, beyond property alone, their 'homes, communities and the personalized meanings they had built around home places' (Ó Tuathail and Dahlman 2006: 246). In the reconciliation period, too, the 1995 Dayton Accords separated once diverse landscapes into ethnically singular zones, recasting and subsequently displacing social, cultural and historical landscapes of home built over generations. This was a home destruction that reached beyond the destruction of dwellings and displacement of people, to the erasure of a sense of historical connection to the homeland and a feeling of inability to rebuild home long after the period of conflict has ended.

In geographer Christopher Harker's (2009) research focusing on Palestinian displacement, domicide too is harnessed to understand the intentional destruction of home beyond the loss of, or removal from, the dwelling alone. For one participant interviewed, the loss of the familial home his father had built not only brought about domicide in the loss of a physical site of security, but also deprived him of a sense of future stability for himself and his family. For Harker's participant, home and its loss is 'not simply a set of spatial relations in and of the (temporal) present, but also a set of relations extending towards the future' (2009: 326). In both instances, although the loss of, or displacement from, the material home may be the initial locus of grief, the domicidal impact felt through such loss moves far beyond the four walls of the house, and into wider social, symbolic and temporal conceptualisations of home. Although these socio-symbolic elements have been touched upon in the research just discussed, further insight regarding the implications of socio-symbolic domicide across a wider set of contexts and subjects is vital in extending academic understanding of the many and varied consequences of the intentional destruction of home. The destruction of home through war is a crucial area of study. But the more mundane, so-called everyday ways in which people's homes are destroyed remains less researched. This is something that this book seeks to redress through a focus on the mobilisation of domicide through UK housing policy and legislation.

## Agents of domicide: stigma and precarity in housing policy

In the context of this book, I am primarily concerned with the relationship between domicide and class.[1] Through the analysis of political speeches, interviews with social tenants, families who have experienced homelessness, squatters and other key stakeholders, and my attendance at a range of protests, conferences and political rallies over the last nearly ten years, I examine how domicide manifests time and again as a phenomenon that is deeply rooted in class inequality. Through the targeted destruction of the homes of low-income and working-class people, justified through austerity rhetoric, the class-based nature of domicide is writ large throughout the examples of this book. The bedroom tax, an unregulated private rented sector and promotion of temporary accommodation policies, and the criminalisation of squatting are clearly domicidal in that they deliberately destroy people's homes and/or homemaking capacities in the long term.

Although I focus on the relationship between housing, domicide and class in the context of the UK, and specifically London, this is far from a solely British phenomenon. Government policies across the globe are regularly framed around a moralistic rhetoric that encourages and supports particular kinds of homes and households, and deters and denounces others. This state dictation of what a home should be is governance at its most intimate, producing hierarchical structures that instruct people on how to conduct the most personal aspects of their lives. There is a wide range of examples the world over of intimate governance enacted through the homespace, with varying degrees of explicitness. For example, housing policy in Singapore specifically prioritises state housing for those who are considered to have a 'proper family nucleus' – reducing homemaking options for the many single male working–class migrants who work in the city-state. Through the site of the homespace, Singaporean housing policy explicitly rewards those it deems to be living 'appropriately', and inhibits the lives of those it does not (Oswin 2010). On the other side of the world, local governments in the USA, in flagrant disregard of the 1968 Fair Housing Act, focus the development of public housing in existing ghettoes rather than more affluent areas, thus furthering social and racial segregation (Robinson 1995; *The New York Times* 2015). Residents are divided and defined by the geography and tenure of their homes and neighbourhoods, the spaces in which they conduct their everyday lives constructed through governance strategies that racially and socially discriminate them through the medium of the homespace.

In the UK context, citizens are encouraged to form homes and households that are in keeping with normative neoliberal ideologies of family life. Married couples are rewarded with tax breaks, and 'troubled families' associated with welfare dependency, addiction and crime are framed as a growing national crisis that must be curbed by government intervention (Cameron 2011b; Wilkinson 2013). UK government policies across the political spectrum have long revolved around the stringent governance of those it deems to be 'troubled' (namely the poor and/or those in receipt of welfare), and the implementation of a moralising agenda enacted through the homespace. Processes of gentrification dispossess working-class people of their homes to make way for high-value housing and wealthy tenants in the name of urban 'regeneration' and neighbourhood improvement (Kallin 2011; Campkin 2013; Watt 2013; Kallin and Slater 2014; Minton 2017). The rise of urban regeneration policies that explicitly target the demolition of council estates and displace their residents is particularly emblematic of the state-led and class-based nature of domicide. Gentrification once referred to a steady stream of middle-class, bohemian types into low-income inner-city neighbourhoods (Lees 2000). Now, as scholars such as Loretta Lees, Tom Slater, Anna Minton and Paul Watt have traced in detail, gentrification has, over the past several decades, become a purposeful, streamlined policy practice: this is what has been termed by Watt and others as 'state-led gentrification' (Lees 2000; Lees et al 2013; Watt 2013; Minton 2017). This evolved iteration of gentrification is predicated on legitimising the large-scale displacement and dispossession of working-class and low-income people. This is able to occur when the domicidal nature of such policies becomes shrouded in narratives that demonise the people being slowly pushed out of their homes.

The examples of state-led domicidal policies and their legitimisation described above are able to occur through two interrelated processes. First, the application of what the sociologist Imogen Tyler terms 'stigma power' (2020). Stigma power emphasises stigma as structural as well as individual – and indeed it is the structural elements that feed individual experiences of stigma. As Tyler and Slater note, it is a 'classificatory form of power' (2018: 722) – an important means of establishing and defining inequality through the affixation of particular people with markers of shame. These markers can be literal, the most brutal and visceral example being the branding of enslaved African people by Europeans during the long era of chattel slavery. As Tyler notes, in this context stigma marks 'functioned as a visual form of identification' (2020: 12). However, this affixation can also be more symbolically embedded through tropes associated with maligned groups. In the case of the British class system, this relates to entrenching ideas of working-class people as abject through an array of stereotypes. For example, there is a well-established characterisation of people in receipt of benefits as day-drinking, tracksuit-wearing slobs – stereotypes made popular through television characters such as Harry Enfield's Wayne and Waynetta Slob, and Matt Lucas's Vicky Pollard.

In the context of housing policy, stigma is utilised by governments to categorise people on the basis of who is and is not deserving of home. Those deemed abject, feckless or unproductive become fair game in austerity politics – scapegoated as responsible for national economic hardship, the curtailment of their rights to home becomes easier to justify. Simultaneously, particular kinds of homes are narrativised as undesirable and in need of reform. The sociologist Lois Wacquant (2007) considers these spatial aspects of stigma through what he terms 'territorial stigmatisation'. Territorial stigmatisation is the purposeful deployment of rhetoric that equates degenerating housing conditions with the degeneracy of their residents (Slater and Anderson 2012; Slater 2013). This is a process of obscuring structural failings such as state disinvestment in particular (read: social, low-income) housing and neighbourhoods, instead constructing narratives of antisocial and abject behaviour as the reason for poor-quality homes (Sisson 2020). Stigma and territorial stigmatisation are cornerstones of domicide, with anti-working-class narratives used time and again by politicians and policymakers to justify stripping away rights to home.

A second concept that is foundational to the legitimisation of class-based domicide is precarity. Most contemporary academic understandings of precarity are foregrounded in the works of polemic feminist political theorists such as Judith Butler and Lauren Berlant. Butler (2009) calls for a social ontology of precariousness, whereby we understand *precariousness* as an innate human condition, one that emanates from our very sociability as human beings. They argue that *precarity*, on the other hand, is a politically induced process forged through power relations and governance practices: the exploitation of precariousness for the benefit of some and at the expense of others (Butler 2009). In their book *Frames of War*, Butler considers the ways in which depictions of modern warfare in media and political rhetoric present some lives as more grieveable than others: that along the constructed boundaries of class, gender, race and so forth are forged understandings of who has societal, cultural and political worth, and who does not (Butler 2009). Precarity, then, is a condition constructed through value: that those who experience precarious conditions most acutely do not produce enough worth to mitigate it. This expression of human worth is intrinsically embedded in the structures demarcated by capitalism, for which the concept of (financial) worth is integral.

Berlant further expands upon the structural embeddedness of precarity in their work *Cruel Optimism*, arguing that precarity is inherently intertwined with neoliberal economic practices (Berlant 2011). Capitalism in and of itself is rooted in a reliance on precarity, dependency and risk. Capital is produced through precarity via the mobilisation, and normalisation, of investment in free-market structures that offer the chance to profit from what is uncertain: for example, the private property market. In the neoliberal capitalist context, then, precarity is framed as not only a normalised condition, but as a means of achieving a profitable 'good life' – with its promises of job security, upward mobility and socioeconomic equality (Berlant 2011). The increased privatisation and rolling back of welfare services that occur alongside this form part of what Berlant describes as the 'neoliberal feedback loop' (2011: 192). Precarity is redistributed along class lines as those not engaging in the free-market are constructed as morally unsound and thus deserving of their precarious condition, and those investing in neoliberal economic and social structures are told that their fantasies of the 'good life' will be rewarded.

Precarity remains most widely discussed and analysed as a concept in relation to employment. The economist Guy Standing (2011) has in his work traced the increasing pervasiveness of precarity within labour market structures. He argues that precarity has resulted in the manifestation of the *precariat* as a contemporary working-class category. Standing's work outlines key characteristics of contemporary labour and workforce structures that differentiate the precariat from its predecessors. Unlike the working classes of the pre-deindustrialisation era, whose relationship with labour was commonly associated with high-skilled and long-term industry-based employment that included paid holiday and sick leave and secure pensions, the precariat is made up of people whose long-term work patterns consist of insecure jobs interspersed with regular unemployment (Standing 2011). Such instability has subsequently impacted on other aspects of everyday life, including destabilising access to, and the maintenance of, secure housing.

Particularly in the post-2008 context, precarity has come to permeate almost every aspect of society. As I have argued with Ella Harris in other work, precarity has increasingly moved beyond being normalised, to a condition that is actively celebrated (Harris and Nowicki 2018). For example, Harris (2020) has explored this in relation to the 'pop-up' phenomenon of the 2010s. During this time, short-term shops, bars, restaurants and so on made use of interim sites made vacant by economic downturn. This reframed precarity as indicative of innovation and entrepreneurship, rather than a condition that governments need to work to end. Similarly, and in relation to housing policy, temporary housing has been increasingly recast from a last resort to being actively celebrated (as long as it is a financially lucrative enterprise). As is explored in detail in Chapters 3 and 4, housing typologies such as property guardianships and pop-up social housing schemes are narrativised as positive and pioneering, rather than emblematic of a failing housing system that needs to be fixed.

Stigma and precarity, then, provide the groundwork for domicide to become embedded within housing policy. Through affixing stigmatising markers on working-class people, and normalising, even celebrating, precarity as part of the social landscape, the curtailing of rights to home becomes concealed, repackaged as fairness or as innovation. The next part of this chapter considers the particular ways in which stigma and precarity have been deployed in UK politics to enable domicidal policies over the last half a century or so.

## Lineages of home in neoliberal political rhetoric

In this book, I largely focus on domicide and its implications in the post-2008 austerity era. However, it is important to understand that the decimation of working-class people's rights to home has a lineage that began long before 2008, as this section will outline.

Home and the familial have long been powerful tools in British political rhetoric. The utilisation of the domestic in twenty- and twenty-first-century political narratives has antecedents in the establishment of model settlements in the eighteenth and nineteenth centuries. This was a set of planned neighbourhoods led by prominent leaders of British industrialisation, such as Titus Salt and George Cadbury, and was predicated on the idea that improved living conditions would improve worker productivity. Emphasis lay on higher design and environmental standards in homes, and the provision of social, educational and recreational facilities. Following this, the interwar period saw a major shift in the framing of political agendas, with Liberal and Conservative governments alike focusing on a more domestic-centric approach (Gilbert and Preston 2003). In the wake of the horrors of the First World War, political rhetoric shied away from traditional glorified, masculinised depictions of the nation as a powerful site of international significance. Although still highly gendered, conceptions of the nation-state focused instead on a more feminised political approach, concentrating on house building, domestic consumerism and positioning women, the home and family at the epicentre of strong nation-building in the aftermath of war (Light 1991). This continued in the post-Second World War context, where large-scale social housebuilding projects formed part of a newly emergent welfare state in the UK, and established council housing as a significant tenure. The introduction of the welfare state was one of the most monumental shifts in British society in the twentieth century. The provision of a national health service, state-owned housing and financial support for the unemployed transformed the lives of millions of working-class people. However, as housing scholars Beth Watts and Suzanne Fitzpatrick have explored in depth, the welfare state also brought about the institutionalisation of working-class conditionality – meaning that 'the provision of goods and services by the state or other welfare providers inevitably ... shapes, moulds and constrains the choices people make' (Watts and Fitzpatrick 2018: 3). The establishment of this relationship between the state and working-class people has formed the bedrock of 'deserving versus undeserving' narratives that have perpetuated understandings of class and home ever since. The early to mid-twentieth century therefore saw the beginning of a longstanding and complex relationship between governance, social tenancy and home that is central to the story told in this book.

Rhetorics of home in British political discourse has a rich and multifaceted history that would make a compelling book of its own. However, my focus here is on the 'neoliberal turn' of the 1970s onwards due to its particular significance in the shaping of the domicidal policy and legislative decisions central to this book. Neoliberalism, in the context of this book, should be understood as a dualistic process, whereby the rolling back of the state in favour of free-market principles is espoused, somewhat contradictorily, alongside the heavy-handed use of state power in the sustainment of these principles. The bedroom tax, rising family homelessness and temporary accommodation policies, and the criminalisation of squatting are indicative of such methods that dismiss and debilitate forms of housing that are not market-oriented, and concurrently contribute to the ongoing establishment of free-market logics as common sense through practices of state intervention. These policies reflect both destructive (the rolling back of state welfare) and creative (the rolling out of markets and market logics) processes of neoliberalism identified by Peck and Tickell (2002), enacted specifically through the homespace.

It is not an overstatement to say that Margaret Thatcher's premiership, from 1979 to 1990, brought about huge social and ideological upheaval. While not the originator of neoliberalism, Thatcher was inarguably a key architect in its cultivation as, beyond a presiding ideology, a set of logics without alternative. In relation to home, Thatcher's Conservative governments significantly restructured housing policy during the latter part of the twentieth century, firmly connecting housing tenure to individual and state morality. This refiguration of housing and home in large part underscored existing understandings of social tenants as abject, enabling the domicidal policies of future governments that are the central case studies of this book to come into being. The Thatcher administration(s) were particularly ingenious in their fusing together of economically neoliberal and socially conservative ideals of homemaking. This heralded the rise of contemporary free-market, individualist-focused nation-building, while at the same time retaining home and the nuclear family as central sociopolitical values. Depictions of traditional homemaking in particular remained integral to the Conservative moral project. Indeed, in the early years of her leadership, Thatcher was often portrayed in relation to her role as a wife and mother, famously photographed standing over her kitchen sink doing the dishes in a motherly floral apron. Such imagery explicitly espoused home-as-nation rhetoric, Thatcher's well-maintained home 'a metaphor for the nation' (Gilbert and Preston 2003: 272). Throughout her premiership, Thatcher continually intertwined governance with the familial and homely through a specifically neoliberal lens, in an uneasy yet ultimately successful political performance that paired the encouragement of individual property speculation with traditional homely nuclear family values. Thatcher argued that it was only through individuals' responsibility to build strong familial foundations and a home capable of 'balancing the books' that a secure and successful nation could be maintained, and that an over-reliance on the state leads to a lack of citizen commitment to homemaking on the scales of both the household and the nation. As she stated in an interview with *Woman's Own* in 1987, "most [social] problems will be solved within the family structure" (Thatcher 1987). Homemaking, then, was utilised by Thatcher to conduct a moralising and intimate governance agenda, whereby people were instructed on how to perform appropriately as neoliberal citizens through the homespace. Such constructions were specifically class-oriented, encouraging the working classes to participate in neoliberal frameworks of homemaking that promoted individual responsibility towards the home on the national, as well as the personal, scale. In particular, Thatcher explicitly pitted homeownership against council tenancy as the key to a successful home life, and thus a successful nation.

Thatcher's most notable and era-defining housing policy was the Right to Buy scheme. Introduced in 1980,[2] Right to Buy was a seminal point in the promotion of individualist, anti-welfare rhetoric that has shaped British class politics and understandings of home ever since. Right to Buy encouraged council housing tenants to purchase their homes for a fraction of their market value. Inevitably, those with enough capital were able to transition into private homeownership, with the poorest tending to remain in council housing. This forever altered the social and cultural landscape of home in Britain, and proves a seminal example in understanding the integral role of both homemaking and domicide in governance agendas. Right to Buy made a particular form of homemaking available to those that could afford it, and simultaneously began to dismantle the homemaking capacities of those who could not, thus cementing a consensus of home destruction across class lines. The Right to Buy scheme not only decimated the country's council housing stock, it also furthered the politicisation of tenure type (Blandy and Hunter 2013). Where once council housing had consisted of people of reasonably mixed social and economic backgrounds, their inhabitants inevitably became far more homogeneous in nature, as many wealthier social tenants 'upscaled' to become homeowners (and in many cases later landlords) (Timmins 2001). As the number of homeowners in Britain swelled as a consequence of Right to Buy, homeownership became more explicitly lauded as the desired tenure type. As Thatcher stated in her interview with *Woman's Own*:

'One of the reasons why … we want the spread of personal property ever wider, not only because we want the material benefits to spread further wider, but because we believe when you have that personal property you get a much greater feeling of responsibility because you have to exercise responsibility towards it. … And, you know, there is no such thing as society. There are individual men and women, and there are families. And no government can do anything except through people, and people must look to themselves first.' (Thatcher 1987)

Thatcher's now-infamous "there is no such thing as society" quote reflects her positioning of the home and individual family unit, as opposed to welfare provision, as being at the centre of strong citizenship and nation-building. Here, homeownership is very explicitly moralised, both financially in terms of the home as a site through which both personal and national wealth is constructed, and socially as a means of responsible citizenship.

Right to Buy and Thatcher's focus on the home as a central site of governance therefore established a powerful legacy that intertwined conceptions of the home with the prioritisation of property as a financial product. At the same time, Thatcher's rhetoric continued to connect with socially conservative constructions of ethical citizenship and the promotion of traditional forms of homemaking as lying at the epicentre of a strong nation. All UK governments, Conservative and Labour alike, since Thatcher's have since disseminated a rhetoric that frames homeownership as the aspirational form of tenure, promoting it as beneficial for both the individual and the state (see Flint 2003; Lowe et al 2012; Blandy and Hunter 2013; Hodkinson and Robbins 2013). For the individual, the primary function of the home has been reframed as a financialised space; a source of equity and financial security, particularly in retirement (Smith 2011). For the state, the privately owned home has become a symbol of economic buoyancy and an important site of moral justification for the rolling back of welfare services and the increased penalisation of those in receipt of them. This has occurred hand-in-hand with the increased demonisation of those who cannot or will not aspire to homeownership, in particular social tenants and those that are welfare-dependent more broadly.

As the Thatcher administrations fervently promoted homeownership and the financialisation of home, they simultaneously derided social tenants as unengaged with individualism and wealth creation, the bastions of neoliberal ideology. Right to Buy encouraged binary distinctions between homeowners (or those aspiring to be homeowners) and social tenants, with the latter regarded the antithesis of successful homemaking, and thus successful nation-building (Nowicki 2017). This established a sense of moral justification for the class-driven domicidal policies and agendas which were directed at those who remained in council housing, and in particular those who were also in receipt of other forms of welfare, for example the unemployed. The Right to Buy scheme was therefore central in establishing moralisations of home along the lines of class and tenure that reverberate to this day (Nowicki 2018).

## New Labour, urban decay and the 'underclass'

Although spearheaded by a Conservative prime minister, the class-based moralisation of housing tenure has by no means been limited to Conservative housing policies and rhetoric. Tony Blair's New Labour governments

(1997–2007), in particular, continued to understand housing as a moral concern, whereby social tenancy was further developed as symbolic of what a home *should not* be. In June 1997, the newly elected prime minister gave his inaugural speech at the Aylesbury Estate in Southwark, south London. With the estate[3] as his backdrop, Blair framed his newly formed government as one dedicated to eradicating moral blight and worklessness in the country, stating:

> 'I have chosen this housing estate to deliver my first speech as prime minister for a very simple reason. For eighteen years, the poorest people in our country have been forgotten by government. They have been left out of growing prosperity. ... There is a case not just in moral terms but in enlightened self-interest to act, to tackle what we all know exists – an underclass of people cut off from society's mainstream, without any sense of shared purpose. Now, at the close of the twentieth century, the decline of old industries and the shift to an economy based on knowledge and skills [have] given rise to a new class: a workless class ... a large minority is playing no role in the formal economy, dependent on benefits.' (Blair 1997)

Blair's speech, against the backdrop of the Aylesbury Estate, makes explicit the assumed correlation between social housing,[4] and in particular council estates, and the manifestation of a British 'underclass' – a workshy, politically and socially abject group unequipped to contribute to the neoliberal social order (Welshman 2013). The 1980s onwards saw a rise in academic and popular imaginaries of the council estate-dwelling underclass as a growing threat to a new sociopolitical order that had replaced the industry-centred working classes for a knowledge- and service-based socioeconomic model (Welshman 2013). Derived from Marx's derisive discussions of the 'lumpenproletariat', the concept of the underclass collectivises, as Imogen Tyler puts it, 'an entire plethora of disenfranchised people into one stigmatizing category, denoting dangerousness and expendability' (Tyler 2013: 185). As understandings of the underclass as an (anti)social category were perpetrated through political and public rhetoric throughout this era, social housing was cultivated as the visual and locational centrepiece for this growing moral panic (Tyler 2013). Blair's reference to social tenants as "cut off from society's mainstream" encouraged a common understanding that social housing represented the epicentre of society's ills – a breeding ground for the abject and the dangerous.

This constructed relationship between social housing, and specifically the council estate, and moral degeneracy is territorial stigmatisation writ large. Territorial stigmatisation is perpetuated by events such as Blair's speech at the Aylesbury estate through ongoing connotations that frame council estates as an architectural form within which degenerate social behaviour is inherently inbuilt. Social housing, despite encompassing a wide range of housing and neighbourhood typologies, is most commonly associated with estates – their architectural decay regularly conflated with the supposed moral decay of residents (Tunstall 2020).

Such rhetoric connecting social housing to depictions of a social underclass has further justified the unravelling of rights to home for working-class people by framing domicidal policies as morally necessary and fair. For example, during the 1990s the advent of housing stock transfer from local authorities to housing associations, and the private financing of social housing services through the Private Finance Initiative (PFI), further dismantled social tenants' long-term rights to their homes. Assumptions that the private sector would produce higher quality and more cost-effective housing further justified the erosion of social housing and increased reliance on the private rented sector (Hodkinson 2011; Campkin 2013) – the consequences of which we will explore further in Chapter 3. This, in turn, has contributed to a rise in the urban regeneration projects discussed earlier that in large part demolish social housing estates and decant their residents to make way for profit-bearing property owners and private tenants (Campkin 2013; Lees 2014; Kallin and Slater 2014; Lees and Ferreri 2016). These decisions are narrated as a necessary means of improving a neighbourhood's safety and economic and social appeal. Inherent in these regeneration practices is an understanding that the urban poor are blockades to successful neighbourhoods due to their inherent relationship with crime and degeneracy (Tyler 2013).

More and more, tenure type has been deployed to stratify, exclude and dismiss particular people from the distinctly neoliberal imaginings of home instilled in political rhetoric. The council flat-dwelling, workless underclass in particular has become a firmly established trope in British popular culture. Documentaries such as *Benefits Street, Skint* (Channel 4, 2014 and 2013–15, respectively) and *On Benefits & Proud* (Channel 5, 2013) are high-profile examples of a popularised exclusionary process that frames working-class people as other to the neoliberal project (Crossley and Slater 2014). Such documentaries characterise those in receipt of welfare as 'the bad seeds' of the national family – lazy scroungers who threaten to disrupt the national homespace via a lack of social and economic productivity, and who drain the resources of those that do contribute to the nation. Such societal shaming is not reserved solely for social tenants and people in receipt of welfare. Squatters in contemporary rhetoric are also understood through similar tropes. The popular media, in particular the right-wing tabloid press, regularly portray squatters as hedonistic, dangerous thieves hell-bent on causing destruction to property (more on this in Chapter 4) (Platt 1999; Middleton 2015). Such discourse has therefore cemented a sociopolitical landscape that frames domicidal agendas as morally just, a reasonable consequence for those deemed undeserving of their homes.

## Unravelling home in the Cameron era

During his 2010–16 premiership, David Cameron continued to retain both homemaking and moralised forms of home destruction as central to his administrations' political rhetoric. Such narratives enabled the implementation of stringent welfare reforms – including the bedroom tax – that explicitly penalise the welfare-dependent. Indeed, Cameron presided over some of the most brutal punitive changes to the welfare system since its introduction (Watt and Fitzpatrick 2018). In particular, he installed a programme of stringent conditions that sought to penalise, and in some instances criminalise, people in receipt of benefits deemed to not truly be in need. Sanctions include denial of access to benefits for three years for those who refuse to take up 'reasonable' work, and increasing fines and prison sentences for those found to be cheating the system. As he declared in a speech shortly after his election as prime minister: "When it comes to the sanctions, we're also going to clamp down on those who deliberately defraud the system. No more cautions. We will seek prosecution whenever we can" (Cameron 2011a).

Cameron's government, on the one hand, decimated people's access to benefits, while on the other rewarded those they deemed to be committed to homes and households in keeping with normative neoliberal ideologies. Married couples were granted tax breaks, and same-sex marriage was legalised in 2014 by Cameron's government with much political and social aplomb. In the same period, a programme focusing on 'troubled families' associated with welfare dependency, addiction and crime, moralised such families as responsible for a 'Broken Britain' – a perceived reduction in family values framed as a growing national crisis that must be curbed by government intervention (Cameron 2011b; Wilkinson 2013; Slater 2016a). As the geographer Eleanor Wilkinson notes, 'despite the supposed increasing acceptance of sexual diversity [for example, through the legalisation of same-sex marriage], an exclusionary rhetoric of "family values" continues to circulate' (2013: 206). This inclusion of (some) LGBTQI relationships into normative familial values such as marriage, sits in parallel to the implementation of highly exclusionary and divisive policies such as the bedroom tax and programmes that point to 'troubled families'. These policies are contrastingly framed as responses to the nation's ills, decisions in large part centred around understandings of what a home *should* be. Much like his predecessors, and in particular Thatcher, policies and legislative changes relating to housing and the familial under Cameron were firmly structured around socially conservative understandings of the responsible, self-sustaining nuclear family: married, professional and homeowning (Wilkinson 2013). Such idealised depictions of the home have continued to encourage populist understandings of working-class people as undeserving of home.

Despite the social divisions that his administrations' housing and welfare policies created, Cameron's rhetoric in relation to the domestic conversely promoted unity, with the nation depicted as a home for all. In his 2014 speech to the Conservative Party Conference in Birmingham, Cameron explicitly placed homemaking at the centre of his aspirations for the country's future within the framework of compassionate, one-nation conservatism, asserting his desire to "build a Britain that everyone is proud to call home" (Cameron 2014). Cameron in particular focused on the plight of the poorest in society, declaring:

> 'We are one people in one union and everyone here can be proud of that. ... And here, today, I want to set out how in this generation we can build a country whose future we can all be proud of ... how we can secure a better future for all. How we can build a Britain that everyone is proud to call home. Families come first. They are the way you make a nation strong from the inside out. I care deeply about those who struggle to get by ... we are on your side, helping you be all you can.' (Cameron 2014)

Here, Cameron emphasises desire for a singular, unified national homespace, secured through strong familial structures and overseen by a paternalist and compassionate Conservative government. In the speech, Cameron places particular emphasis on unity, belonging ("we are one people") and social security ("we can secure a better future for all"), evoking well-established (if grossly oversimplified) affectations of home as 'ours', a sacrosanct site of safety and security to be prioritised and protected. Cameron also focuses on the familial as an integral means of state construction, the foundation of "a nation strong from the inside out". Cameron's political rhetoric is clearly founded in homemaking discourse, constructing a sense of unified nation-building and explicitly framing the home and family as the key to a prosperous and secure state. This is further exemplified by Cameron's incorporation of homely imagery during his 2015 re-election campaign, when he conducted an intimate interview with the BBC from the kitchen of his Cotswolds home (BBC 2015). The interview depicts Cameron as an 'average family man' character, cheering his son on at a football match on the village common, and preparing a meal in his rustic country kitchen (very much mirroring the photographs of his predecessor, Thatcher, discussed earlier). Here, Cameron explicitly brings the intimacies of home life to the fore of political rhetoric, his interview implicitly assuring his potential electorate that his continued leadership will be one centred on traditional values of homemaking.

Alongside his cosy espousals of homeliness, Cameron's rhetoric has also continued along a by now well-established trajectory that attributes social tenancy and worklessness to moral decay. His compassionate, homely one-nation speeches also include decidedly othering language that seeks to reinforce the moralisation of home destruction along classed lines. Interlaced throughout many of Cameron's calls for compassion, social unity and constructions of the nation-as-home are numerous references that allude specifically to supporting those who "want to get on and *work hard* in life" (Cameron 2015), those "who do the right thing, put the effort in, who work and build communities" (Cameron 2014), and promises "to be a One Nation government with *working* people at its heart" (Cameron 2015), implicitly condemning people who are unemployed, regardless of their circumstances. Therefore, within the homely imagery of compassionate governance that seeks to maintain and protect a national homespace for all, the workless other is simultaneously framed as unwilling to participate, a deviant figure who chooses not to contribute to national homemaking agendas, and is thus framed as undeserving of rights to home. Such othering again re-establishes conceptions of those who are in receipt of welfare as socially immoral. This, in turn, reinforces justification for the implementation of home-unmaking policies such as the bedroom tax and wider welfare reforms that fixate on the penalisation of people living in social housing and those in receipt of welfare.

This process of homely and familial rhetoric emphasises unity while simultaneously excluding particular groups of people and dismantling their homemaking capacities. This again highlights the complex, and at times contradictory, relationship between rhetorics of home and the realities of housing policy. Cameron's avowal of creating 'a Britain everyone is proud to call home', alongside his consistent references to one-nationism and the unity of British people, stands in stark contrast to the realities of many of the policies implemented under his premiership (Nowicki 2018). On the one hand, Cameron earnestly promised to support the most vulnerable and ensure a morally just society that protects all those who want to "get on in life". On the other, his government(s) introduced a suite of policy reforms that have fundamentally destabilised the homemaking capacities of hundreds of thousands of Britain's most economically and socially vulnerable.

### *Continuing the legacy of the moralised home: from Brexit to COVID-19*

While the majority of the experiences recounted in the following chapters are a direct consequence of policies and legislation implemented by David Cameron's governments, the manipulation and moralisation of home continues to play an integral role in British politics and policymaking.

For much of the last five years, the UK's drawn-out withdrawal from the European Union was near-constant headline news. 2016 was the year that just over 15 million people voted to leave the EU, 'Brexit' became the Oxford English Dictionary's word of the year, and David Cameron walked away from Downing Street whistling while chaos reigned as a consequence of his referendum. Much of the often extremely pernicious language of Brexit, spearheaded by figures such as the former UKIP leader Nigel Farage, centred on 'taking back control' of UK borders. To return to William Walters' term domopolitics, protection of the homeland from a dangerous other was embedded in Brexit rhetoric from the outset. Cameron's referendum opened a floodgate of anti-foreigner and racist sentiment that continued to be cultivated by his successor Theresa May. As the sociologist Teresa Piacentini has observed:

> Brexit means Brexit means go home. That seems to be the dominant message of the new Conservative government under Theresa May, which is reinforcing this interpretation with a stream of proposed policies that range from the requirement that employers list foreign workers, to passport checks on pregnant women in maternity hospitals, and changes to the school census that require the collection of data on pupils' country of birth and nationality. (2016: 57)

The rise in policies that intertwine criminal and immigration law has been termed 'crimmigration' by legal scholars, and continues Cameron's legacy of introducing increasingly punitive legislation targeting those deemed undeserving. Through a focus on crimmigration policies, the British homeland becomes a space hostile to groups of people not in keeping with the neoliberal project – for example, low-income people and (non-Anglophone, non-white) immigrants. As Piacentini also notes, this weaponisation of home as a process of exclusion and erasure was a continuation of May's previous role as home secretary, where she purposefully and publicly established a 'hostile environment' towards supposedly irregular immigrants. This included the infamous 'Go Home' vans, which paraded the streets of Britain bearing banners warning illegal immigrants to 'go home' or face arrest. Whereas Cameron had intermingled exclusionary language alongside his espousals of one-nationism, May's political use of home, both as home secretary and prime minister, was full-throttle in its violent othering of those deemed as not belonging in the UK – in this instance largely non-white and non-Anglophone migrants.

Interestingly, May's own attempt at constructing a cosy domestic image backfired when she was interviewed at home by the *Sunday Times* in December 2016. Designed to portray the then-prime minister in a more intimate light as she discussed her childhood and sleepless nights over Brexit, the interview was derailed by an outcry against the leather trousers she wore, which reportedly cost just under £1,000. Nearly three decades after Margaret Thatcher's 'at home' photoshoot, and just over a year after David Cameron's, May's performance of domesticity was conversely savaged on social media, with many accusing her clothing choice as exemplary of her being out of touch with the British public during a time of austerity. This in spite of the fact that, unlike the hyper-privileged former Etonian and Bullingdon Club member Cameron, May, like Thatcher before her, comes from relatively humble roots. The enraged response at her attempts to portray a domesticated side perhaps reflects an outcry against austerity – depictions of a lavish home life igniting anger as so many people's homes have been decimated by welfare cuts, reductions in average pay and the rising cost of living. However, it should be noted that many of these policies – including those that are central to this book – were implemented and overseen by David Cameron, whose own 'at home' interview had taken place just over a year earlier, and yet who received none of the ire experienced by Theresa May. This points to a gendered moralisation of the home, this time by the public and the media rather than politicians, that scorns wealthy, childless women in particular as undeserving of their perceived extravagances (in this case a pair of overpriced trousers). This serves as a further iteration of the ways in which the home functions as a powerful tool through which those deemed unconforming are moralised and derided. The former prime minister may not be a social tenant, or a non-white migrant, but her ill-judged attempted display of domesticity revealed her to be another figure seen as not in keeping with the idealised home: a childless, ageing woman.

### Stay at home: the role of the domestic during the COVID-19 pandemic

As I was writing this book, home became unexpectedly central to political agendas across the globe. Following the outbreak of the coronavirus pandemic at the start of 2020, almost every nation in the world imposed some form of lockdown to curb the spread of the virus. In the UK, there were three lockdowns in 2020 and 2021 ordering residents to 'stay at home', and for the majority of the pandemic 'working from home where possible' was the official government guideline. Practically overnight it became almost universal for homes to be stretched to encompass virtually every aspect of our lives: our homes became our workplaces, our schools, our entertainment centres. But after a decades-long campaign to dismantle decent affordable housing for any that are not homeowners, and the decimating impact of the austerity era, for many people it quickly became clear that their homes were not equipped to encompass such widening of its function. For so many, 'stay at home' was akin to a prison sentence, trapped in cramped, poor-quality, insecure accommodation with nowhere to go. It is grimly predictable that these were the same people who are also more vulnerable to the virus itself. As well as overcrowded accommodation having obvious disadvantages when faced with a highly contagious disease, people living in these conditions are also more likely to have existing health issues and jobs that mean they cannot work from home. Indeed, research by Inside Housing revealed a stark correlation between overcrowding and the COVID-19 death rate. Their analysis revealed that the London boroughs of Newham and Brent, the two most overcrowded local authorities in the country, had the two highest death rates across England and Wales during the first months of the pandemic (Barker 2020).

During the first lockdown in particular, then-Prime Minister Boris Johnson and then-Health Secretary Matt Hancock regularly implored people who had caught COVID-19 to sleep in separate rooms and use separate bathrooms from their families in order to avoid infecting members of their household. Later on, as the country moved into spring, gardens became increasingly central in suggestions of how to entertain yourself and your family at home. This further revealed the huge gap in an imagined 'property-owning democracy' – a Margaret Thatcher phrase resurrected by Johnson – living in spacious, privately owned houses with gardens, and the lived reality of so many people's home lives. Temporary measures such as the 'Everyone In' scheme which in summer 2020 mandated that all rough sleepers should be accommodated, mainly in hotels, to reduce transmission, and a moratorium on private rented sector evictions, suggested at least an understanding from Johnson's government of the importance of shelter during the pandemic. But such policies also reveal the extent of the precarity that is built into UK housing policy, and the fragility of home for low-income (and indeed increasing numbers of middle-income) people. If the pandemic has writ large the importance of home, so too has it laid bare the realities of a housing system hinged on the destruction of so many forms of homemaking.

As COVID-19 has waned in terms of policy importance, if not virulence, the home and domestic continues to be wielded as a narrative device. Johnson's landslide victory in 2019 was in part achieved through turning the so-called 'red wall' of Labour constituencies in the north of England blue. This victory came with promises of 'levelling up' investment in economically deprived areas of the UK. 'Missions' asserted by the newly renamed Department for Levelling Up, Housing and Communities in a February 2022 White Paper included halving the number of poor-quality rented housing and rejuvenating 'run down' town centres and communities (Department for Levelling Up, Housing and Communities 2022). Although these promises have remained largely empty rhetoric, Michael Gove, the former Secretary of State for Levelling Up and Housing, made some headway in addressing the ever-growing issue of poor-quality homes in the UK. Gove introduced the Social Housing (Regulation) Bill (currently being considered in the House of Lords) which aims to better regulate and punish unscrupulous social landlords. His department also published a 'Fairer Private Rented Sector' White Paper in June 2022, which includes plans to abolish no-fault evictions,[5] legally apply the Decent Homes Standard to private renting, and introduce a housing ombudsman in order to improve tenant protection. These measures taken by Gove's department perhaps finally suggested a government in acknowledgement of the decimation of rights to home experienced by so many over the last half century or so. However, in July 2022, Gove was fired by Boris Johnson as part of the former prime minister's final attempts to cling to power. The future of these housing policies under a new Conservative government remains unclear at the time of writing. And so unjust housing conditions continue into whatever new iteration of government awaits. As the remainder of this book will show across its three case studies, through the moralisation of home and positioning of certain, classed figures as being undeserving of it, domicide has become a core component of the UK housing system – the brutal impacts of which continue to resonate and be compounded with every new social, political and economic challenge the country faces.

# 2

# The bedroom tax and diminishing rights to home

This chapter explores the first of the book's three key case studies of socio-symbolic domicide – the removal of the spare room subsidy, better known as the bedroom tax. However, before examining the impact of the policy itself, the chapter provides an overview of the broader context of social tenancy in the UK. I do so as the shifting ways in which social tenants have been framed and imagined over time is crucial in understanding the conception and impact of the bedroom tax.

## Contextualising the bedroom tax: a brief history of social tenancy in the UK

Social housing in Britain was first introduced in the UK in London during the final years of the nineteenth century, and was borne out of the horrendous living conditions of the poor working classes, particularly in the East End of London, where the life expectancy of low-skilled labourers at the time was just 16 (Hanley 2007). The social scientist and philanthropist Charles Booth's seminal *Inquiry into the Life and Labour of the People in London*, a large-scale study of the lives and labour conditions of the city's working classes conducted between 1886 and 1903, brought to public attention the extreme nature of poverty in the capital. It was during this period that the state began to involve itself more in housing provision, and Britain's first council estate was built by the London County Council in 1893 on Boundary Street, between Shoreditch and Bethnal Green (Hanley 2007). However, it was not until the interwar period – and the 1919 Housing and Town Planning Act – that council house building was taken up at any significant scale. In the aftermath of the First World War, council housing was, for the first time, acknowledged as an integral long-term solution to slum housing (Ravetz 2001). The Act provided local councils with subsidies in order to encourage housebuilding, leading to council housing rising from roughly 1 to 10 per cent of the country's total housing stock during the interwar period (Bentley 2008).

Commitment to and investment in council housebuilding grew further during and in the wake of the Second World War. The 1942 'Social Insurance and Allied Services' report, better known as the Beveridge report after its author, the economist William Beveridge, is often cited as the blueprint of the British welfare state, establishing the 'five giants' of want, disease, ignorance, squalor and idleness as a set of evils to be vanquished in the post-war reconstruction of Britain (Timmins 2001). Housing was set to become a particularly urgent and problematic issue in the post-war period, as during the war huge swathes of Britain's housing stock had been destroyed or damaged, particularly in London. Indeed, it is estimated that at its peak, V1 and V2 bombing caused damage to 20,000 homes a day in the capital alone (Calder 1969). Pressure to build affordable housing at high speed was spearheaded by war veterans, many of whom were returning to destroyed homes and neighbourhoods and squalid living conditions, and who subsequently in many cases had little choice but to turn to squatting.[1]

Aneurin Bevan, then–post-war minister for health (under which housing policy was then incorporated), faced consistent pressure to build council housing at a quicker rate than it was being delivered. However, he argued that housing quality and social mixing should be at the core of the new social housing agenda, famously stating: "We shall be judged for a year or two by the *number* of houses we build. We shall be judged in ten years' time by the *type* of houses we build" (quoted in Foot 1973: 127). Bevan extended the minimum standard size for council housing from 750 to 900 square feet, and in 1948 removed pre-war legislative requirements that council housing should only be provided for the working classes, instead placing emphasis on constructing socially mixed communities, where "the doctor, the grocer, the butcher and the farm labourer all lived in the same street" (quoted in Foot 1973: 78).

However Bevan's social utopia did not come to pass, as the demand for ever-faster housebuilding continued to increase. Conservative and Labour governments alike subsequently committed to higher rates of housebuilding, including the development of prefabricated high-rise council blocks and estates – an architecture which has since come to define social housing (Timmins 2001; Hanley 2007). In the wake of the movement towards high quantity rather than high quality homes from the 1960s onwards, the political – both Labour and Conservative – love affair with council housing began to disintegrate. In 1968 a gas explosion caused Ronan Point, a 22-storey prefabricated council building in the London borough of Newham, to partially collapse, killing four people. The disaster became emblematic of increasingly negative perceptions of council housing (Ravetz 2001). Council housing became synonymous with structural and social decay, with council estates and tower blocks in particular becoming associated with high levels of crime and poverty by the 1970s and 80s (see Chapter 1 for more on how this reframing came to pass) (Tyler 2013). Lynsey Hanley, in her astute social history-come-personal memoir of council estate life, remarked of the legacy of high-rise social housing: 'Tower blocks, in the public mind, represent all that is worst about the welfare state: the failure to provide the kind of housing that most people regard as a prerequisite for a happy family life; lack of choice; dependence and isolation. ... And concrete. Ugly concrete' (Hanley 2007: 98).

As public opinion of social housing shifted dramatically during the 1970s, so too did perceptions of their inhabitants. Bevan's vision of council tenancy as a condition of pride and social unification was replaced with contemporary tropes of the 'scrounging' social tenant. Public imaginings of the workshy inhabiting concrete, crime-infested 'no-go' estates became cemented through political rhetoric and the news media, and terms like 'depressed' and 'sink' estates became commonplace (Slater 2018). These increasingly negative perceptions became self-perpetuating, with some estates, particularly those that were high density, becoming difficult to let even to those in acute housing need due to their poor reputation, leading to a rise in empty council homes.[2] Key issues identified at the time were lack of play facilities for children, lack of privacy, high noise levels, unreliable lifts, poor refuse disposal management, and lack of community facilities[3] (Tunstall 2020). The dawn of neoliberal political agendas in the late 1970s and early 1980s, in conjunction with this growing disregard for social housing as a viable and respectable form of tenure, helped to catalyse this shift in popular imaginings of council housing from the bedrock of a socialist utopia to the breeding ground for an abject, criminal and unproductive population (Tyler 2013). This political reimagining was further cemented by the advent of the Right to Buy policy of the early 1980s. As discussed in the previous chapter, Right to Buy encouraged wealthier tenants to purchase their council homes for a large discount. The policy therefore formalised perceptions of council tenancy that had been developing throughout the previous decade as something that should be escaped from, rather than as the housing for life intended by Bevan. Council housing and its tenants became increasingly residualised from this period – imagined as poverty traps inhabited by a social underclass (Welshman 2013).

Right to Buy was followed by another dramatic shift in the council housing system: the rise of housing associations. In the wake of disinvestment in council housing, the 1988 Housing Act encouraged the extension of housing associations into social housing provision. This essentially meant that the private sector suddenly had a large role in the design, procurement and management of social housing.[4] The Act enabled them to essentially operate as private-sector companies by borrowing money and investing as private-sector entities (Hodkinson 2012; Atkinson and Jacobs 2016). From the 1990s onwards, large swathes of council housing stock were voluntarily transferred to housing associations, with many council tenant groups voting *en masse* to become housing association residents. Such decisions were largely made due to tenant dissatisfaction with longstanding disinvestment in council housing by local authorities (Hanley 2007; Mullins 2010). By 2008, 50 per cent of local authorities had transferred their stock to housing associations (Pawson and Mullins 2010). According to the social geographer Stuart Hodkinson, such strategies were deliberately divisive on the part of the Conservative Party (Hodkinson 2012). Hodkinson argues that the government saw strong public housing as a threat to their ambitions to encourage homeownership as the desired form of tenure. Disinvestment in public housing would therefore encourage constructions of homeownership as the sole aspirational form of housing. He also suggests that the dismantling of a strong and autonomous social housing movement removed Conservative opposition, as social housing tenants are a traditionally Labour-leaning sector of the electorate (Hodkinson 2012). Arguably, therefore, the rise of housing associations further contributed to negative sociopolitical constructions of social tenancy in the long term, making explicit understandings of council housing as a failing tenure and therefore in need of assistance from the (quasi) private sector.

This encroachment of the private sector into public housing was also reflective of a wider mass restructuring of the welfare state during this time that saw the increasing privatisation of public services. The PFI was introduced by John Major's Conservative government in 1992, and significantly ramped up during Blair's time as prime minister. The PFI created a new procurement model whereby the design, construction and maintenance of public services and infrastructure (including social housing, the NHS and schools) were outsourced to the private sector (for example, developers and large international banks). These companies invest initial capital through loans, which the public service repays over a period of time (Hodkinson and Essen 2015). This was a huge reimagining of the welfare state, including social housing, as a profit-making enterprise – a fundamental shift that continues to this day and has led to many public services being crippled by debt repayments.[5]

Indeed, over time, and particularly in the wake of the 2008 recession and subsequent austerity agenda, housing associations have become increasingly driven by the private housing market, building properties for market rent and sale, as well as social housing (Mullins 2010; Dorling 2014). The rise of housing associations has also provoked a further shift in conceptions of social housing and the welfare state more broadly. Where once the state had been framed as a source of social provision, rhetoric shifted to one of an 'enabling state'. Since the 1980s, social housing has fallen under this remit. As Hanley notes: 'Housing associations are ... seen as enablers, whereas local authorities will forever be seen as dependency-encouraging providers. ... The suggestion is that local authorities, which once housed half of us, will one day house none of us, and that we had better be prepared' (2007: 145).

The advent of Right to Buy and, later, housing associations, therefore promoted the understanding that social housing is something that should be moved on from. Those who remain are constructed as static, caught in a state of arrested development whereby limited social productivity has led to an inability to attain the more desirable tenure type of homeownership. Therefore, in a sociopolitical climate that derides social tenancy as symbolic of an unproductive societal underclass, policies such as the bedroom tax that specifically target social tenants have been established with relative ease. The precaritisation of social housing, a once highly secure tenure, has been legitimised as morally sound – as finally challenging a scrounging underclass. Indeed, the Department for Work and Pensions' assertion that the bedroom tax had been introduced in order to bring social rents 'in line with the private rented sector' only furthers an understanding that market rates are the 'true' measure of housing value (Department for Work and Pensions 2014). Social tenants, whose housing conditions do not comply with neoliberal understandings of worth, have subsequently seen their rights to home vastly diminished, as the remainder of this chapter will explore.

## Introducing the bedroom tax

The bedroom tax (officially titled the removal of the spare room subsidy) is one of a suite of measures introduced by the Coalition government as part of the 2012 Welfare Reform Act. Borne out of the aftermath of financial recession and the emergence of a social, political and economic discourse centred on austerity rhetoric, the controversial Act instigated a brutal overhaul of the British welfare system. The Act included measures such as stringent work capability assessments for those in receipt of employment support allowance (ESA) and mandatory contributions to council tax regardless of household income. The bedroom tax comprises the flagship housing element of the Act, signalling a significant shift in welfare governance and reconstituting the boundaries of what is an appropriate amount of space in the social housing context. Then-Secretary of State for Work and Pensions Iain Duncan Smith framed the decision to implement the bedroom tax as one based around fairness and tenure equality with the private rented sector. This meant that the policy was introduced within a framework whereby privately owned and rented housing is considered the norm, and social housing an outdated outlier.

The bedroom tax affects social tenants (excluding pensioners) in receipt of housing benefit or the Universal Credit housing element, reducing the amount of housing benefit for tenants deemed to have one or more 'spare bedroom' – 14 per cent for one bedroom, 25 per cent for two or more. The bedroom tax allows for one bedroom per person or couple living as part of the household, with some exceptions, including foster carers, students and members of the armed services who are away and intend to return home (Department for Work and Pensions 2013). While the policy applies to all four UK nations, both the devolved governments of Scotland and

Northern Ireland chose to fully offset the income loss, meaning that in the vast majority of cases social tenants in these two countries are not impacted by the bedroom tax.

## From controversy to apathy: initial responses to the bedroom tax

Shortly after its announcement by the Department for Work and Pensions, the removal of the spare room subsidy's official title became largely obscured, and it has since been known as the 'bedroom tax'. This was much to the consternation of David Cameron, who stated: "I don't accept the bedroom tax is a tax – it's an issue about benefit" (Brown 2013a). The Labour Party's Lord Best, who is said to have coined the term, responded by arguing that 'if you have to pay a sum of money and you can't escape from doing so, and that sum of money goes to the government – it looks to me all very much like having a tax' (Brown 2013b). The policy's popular renaming helped to cement negative public feeling towards it. The use of the word 'bedroom' conjures up imagery of an aspect of home most associated with intimacy and the private. The bedroom connotes many intensely personal activities in human life: it is where we sleep, where we have sex, where we retreat in order to be alone, where we ready ourselves for the day, where we recover when we are unwell. Policies that explicitly regulate this part of our lives are therefore more likely to conjure public outrage. The phrase the 'bedroom tax' has also been compared to, and evoked memories of, the much maligned Conservative taxation of the late 1980s and early 1990s, the 'poll tax'[6] (Perkins 2013). Much like the bedroom tax, the poll tax is an infamous instance of Conservative policy that many argued explicitly targeted the poor and working classes through the disproportionate taxation of larger, usually working-class, households. The bedroom tax, therefore, gained traction as a controversial and invasive policy before it had even been implemented, and the impact of its introduction fully realised.

The bedroom tax also proved immediately controversial due to its disproportionate impact on disabled people. Multiple rooms are often crucial for disabled people whose conditions mean they need to sleep in separate rooms from their partners, or store specialist equipment or medication. According to research by Suzanne Moffat and colleagues (2016), around a third of all social tenants affected by the policy are disabled.[7] From the outset, the charity sector also expressed strong concerns regarding the impact of the bedroom tax on vulnerable and disabled people. Major housing charities such as Shelter and the Joseph Rowntree Foundation published reports that in particular highlighted this disproportionate impact of the policy on disabled people (Webb 2013; Wilcox 2014). Cases such as that of the Carmichaels,[8] widely reported at the time, brought to public attention components of the bedroom tax that directly discriminated against disabled home lives.[9]

Shortly after its introduction, concerns regarding the bedroom tax were also voiced by high-profile international figures and organisations. In December 2013, following an inspection into the UK's adherence to human rights regulations, then-United Nations Special Rapporteur for Housing Raquel Rolnik published a report expressing concern that the bedroom tax was having a negative effect on many of England and Wales' most vulnerable residents. She referred to it as a retrogressive policy, leaving those affected in the precarious position of either struggling to stay in their homes by reducing other living costs such as food and clothing, or having no choice but to leave the homes where they had 'raised their children and lived their lives' (Rolnik 2013: 13). She also noted the 'tremendous despair' felt by many social tenants affected, and recommended that the policy be re-examined in light of emerging data that suggested little budgetary benefit, low moving rates of affected tenants, and growing rent arrears (Rolnik 2013). Rolnik's visit and subsequent report were met with outrage from Conservative politicians and the right-wing press. Then-Conservative housing minister Grant Shapps responded to Rolnik's recommendations by accusing her of political bias. He went so far as to write a letter to then-UN Secretary General Ban Ki-Moon demanding an investigation of her visit, and denouncing Rolnik's recommendation that the bedroom tax be repealed as 'an absolute disgrace' (Shapps 2013). Infamous British right-wing tabloid the *Daily Mail* published a series of outraged pieces on Rolnik, referring to her as a 'loopy Brazilian leftie' (Chorley 2013), 'Brazil nut' (Chapman 2013), and 'revealing' that she stayed in a £300 per night hotel room during her visit (Doughty 2013). This near-hysterical response was perhaps an indication of already-waning public and political demand for the repeal of the bedroom tax.

The Labour Party has generally positioned itself as against the bedroom tax, with past leaders of the opposition Ed Miliband (2010–15) and Jeremy Corbyn (2015–20) promising to repeal the policy in the event of their election to government. However, more recently the party leadership's interest in explicitly condemning it has diminished. While a pledge to repeal the bedroom tax remains in Labour's most recent housing manifesto (2019), current leader (at the time of writing) Keir Starmer is yet to publicly denounce the policy and explicitly continue such commitment to its abolishment. What was once a highly criticised policy, eliciting public outrage, has now drifted from memory – what the journalist Frances Ryan terms a 'political amnesia'. Writing in 2019, she argues that, particularly in an era of 'Brexit-mania', the lived realities of Cameron's austerity agenda have been left by the wayside. What once resulted in public anger and empathy is now a concern of the past – except for those who continue to live with the crippling effects of the bedroom tax and other 'welfare reform' policies, that is. Ryan's powerful observation has, of course, become all the more relevant in the context of COVID-19, where Brexit-mania was replaced by pandemic-mania. Meanwhile, a decade after its introduction, the bedroom tax continues to quietly disrupt and dismantle people's home lives. The remainder of this chapter is dedicated to bringing back to light some of the stories of those impacted by the devastating policy, and the ways in which it has eroded their rights to home. In so doing, it hopes to shake off some of the political amnesia Ryan identifies.

## Slow violences: the fear of eviction

Perhaps the most expected impact of the bedroom tax in relation to home destruction is the threat of rent arrears and forced eviction. For social tenants affected by the bedroom tax, forced eviction is not a given outcome of the policy, but it is nonetheless a looming spectre, a fear embedded into their everyday lives. This is because the policy almost inevitably leads to rent arrears, as many tenants are no longer able to pay their rent in full due to loss of housing benefit income. Indeed, several participants told me that being subject to the bedroom tax had led them to fall into rent arrears for the first time in their lives. Rather than immediately forcibly evicting people from their homes (a topic that will be discussed further in Chapter 4 in relation to squatting), the bedroom tax disempowers people's relationships with their homes through stripping away their sense of belonging, security and comfort, traditionally understood to be the pillars of an ideal home life (Relph 1976; Blunt and Dowling 2006). Tenants are left in a position whereby the homes they may have lived in for decades under the premise of secured lifetime tenancies have been transformed into sites of insecurity and financial strain.

This was highlighted as a primary concern by some of the housing association and housing charity employees that I interviewed. Amy, a housing officer whose role was jointly funded by a large national housing association and an inner London local authority, ran a drop-in advice service for local residents at the time the bedroom tax came into effect. The drop-in was run in a local community centre and hosted a range of charities and other support services, including surgeries with a housing solicitor and the constituency's local councillors and MP. I joined Amy at the drop-in centre in late 2014 to discuss what, if any, changes she had noticed in the aftermath of the Welfare Reform Act. I was particularly interested to know whether the reasons for people attending the drop-in had changed in the wake of the Act's implementation. She told me what she had been most struck by was the increasing number of people who were now coming in for advice on how to deal with mounting debt. She commented that most people she had spoken to who were affected by the bedroom tax did not want to leave their homes or local area due to strong emotional ties and support networks, but that many could no longer afford to live in the borough without falling into high levels of debt.

Amy noted that although there had been an increase in people coming in for advice in relation to the bedroom tax, this had peaked immediately after the policy had been introduced in 2012 before beginning to decline. Amy understood this to be because people were either receiving financial support in the form of Discretionary Housing Payment (DHP),[10] or were trying to cope on their own. However, she suspected that 'coping' often meant continuing to fall into arrears, with people unable to avoid indebtedness due to low incomes and high living costs. Even where tenants are accessing DHP, this form of impact prevention is ultimately unsustainable as DHP funding has been cut most years since 2013 – including by £40million between 2013 and 2015. And although DHP funding was boosted from £139.5 million in 2019 to £180 million in 2020 in light of the pandemic, this has since been slashed by 22 per cent.

This close to year-on-year reduction in DHP, and tenants learning to live with indebtedness indicates that the impacts of the bedroom tax are not always acute, but rather are indicative of what the humanities scholar Rob Nixon (2013) has termed 'slow violence' – an erasure of security and rights to home that is gradual – a trickling away, rather than a spectacular, all-at-once destruction. Awareness of the ramifications of these slow, long-term effects was echoed in my conversation with the principal solicitor for a major national housing charity, where he expressed deep concerns about the long-term financial ramifications for social tenants falling into rent arrears as a consequence of the bedroom tax. He worried that DHP would act as something of a cloak for the true impact of the bedroom tax, which would not be felt for many years. This is perhaps one of the most pernicious ways in which the bedroom tax, and 'welfare reform' more generally, work – not by clearly and instantaneously tearing people from their homes, but rather by slowly destroying them, piece by piece, over long periods of time. This war of attrition against rights to home can be seen in the further impacts of the bedroom tax discussed in the remainder of this chapter.

## Destroying a sense of home

The bedroom tax has clear financial implications that establish insecurity through the threat of forced eviction. But the story of the bedroom tax and its impact is not one of financial hardship and insecurity alone. It is also a story of the dismantling of domestic security for people who are often already vulnerable. It is a story of precarity seeping into the everyday lived experience of social tenants affected, who are left not only struggling to pay their rent, but struggling to remain in homes that have been adapted to suit their needs, struggling to remain in neighbourhoods that contain friend and family support networks, and struggling to justify their position as social tenants in a political landscape that equates social housing with social blight.

Jane's experience exemplifies these compounding forms of home destruction. She moved into her council flat in north London in the early 1980s. She had previously been renting privately, but decided to move into the, at the time, more expensive council property to ensure a more secure future for herself and her two children due to the promise of a lifetime tenancy – a huge perk that, until recently, council housing provided. She was particularly grateful for this tenure security, as she had suffered from a severe form of arthritis since her twenties that has gradually worsened over time, leaving her unable to work full-time. One of her daughters has cystic fibrosis, a condition that vastly reduces her ability to work due to regular and extended periods spent in hospital. Jane therefore not only lives with a chronic health condition herself, but acts as her daughter's carer. Since 2013, Jane has been subject to the bedroom tax and, for the first time in her life, almost immediately fell into rent arrears. According to the Department for Work and Pensions, the box room where she keeps her daughter's medication, wheelchair and other medical equipment is considered 'spare'.

I had initially made contact with Jane when I posted on a housing association's tenants and residents' association online forum. When I met Jane in a cafe near her flat in 2014, she told me that she had decided to speak to me as she was tired of the bad press social tenants had been subject to in recent years. Initially, our conversation was somewhat stilted and awkward, with Jane appearing reluctant to answer my questions, and visibly balking when I asked her how the bedroom tax had impacted her, asking me defensively whether what I was really asking was how much debt she was in. It was only after I hastily explained that that was not what I had meant at all, that she was in no way obliged to answer anything I asked her, and that I understood to some extent what she was going through as a family member of mine had also been affected by the bedroom tax, that she began to warm up and share her story. Later on in our meeting, she apologised for how she had initially reacted to my question, explaining that, as a social tenant, she felt that she had to constantly be on the defensive. She commented that she had felt this particularly acutely since the Coalition government had been formed in 2010, and referred to their austerity agenda as a 'propaganda campaign' against social tenants that had begun as soon as the election had been won. Since noticing this shift in political rhetoric, Jane had become understandably concerned about how other people viewed her, and felt she was under constant public scrutiny. She felt that, as a social tenant in a desirable part of inner London, she is now seen to be occupying valuable property that she has not earned. Essentially, she felt that others judged her as undeserving of her home: "There's an attitude of 'these people shouldn't be here because it's [her flat] worth too much'. ... But it's not just bricks and mortar, it's my home! Just because I don't own it, it doesn't mean it's not mine."

Jane's experience of the bedroom tax was one that had destabilised her sense of having any right to her home. Her comments highlight the concerning way in which rights to home are so commonly understood as being synonymous with legal and financial property ownership (Lowe et al 2012; Madden and Marcuse 2016). For Jane, lack of legal ownership did not equate to a lack of ownership full stop. She has lived in her flat for decades, raised her children there, formed relationships with her neighbours, and adapted her home to suit her needs. The importance of her home in her identity construction and sense of self is no less because she is a social tenant rather than a homeowner. This is something that is fundamentally ignored by a social and political narrative that frames social tenancy as something to move on from rather than a legitimate form of homemaking in its own right.

Disempowerment and the fear of losing one's home was a common theme in my meetings with social tenants impacted by the bedroom tax. When I met Vas in 2014 she had lived in her north-west London council house for over two decades. She lives with a musculoskeletal disorder, is predominantly housebound and relies on a walking stick to move around. As a result of her condition, Vas had not worked for many years. Her partner worked as a part-time handyman and, prior to the bedroom tax, they had been managing to pay their rent, albeit with very little income remaining after bills, food and other essentials. She became subject to the bedroom tax as one of her adult children left home, leaving her with a spare room. Like Jane, the policy's implementation left her in rent arrears for the first time, and when we met she was concerned about the long-term implications of this.

Vas discussed the sense of disempowerment she felt in the wake of the policy's implementation. She was unequivocal that her housing situation was noticeably worse under the Coalition government. Vas was particularly keen to raise the subject of Iain Duncan Smith, the controversial then-Secretary of State for the Department for Work and Pensions. She referred to the bedroom tax as being: "Iain Duncan Smith's personal agenda ... this is the reason the bedroom tax is happening now. ... They're [the Coalition] trying to push the poor out of London." Indeed, as Frances Ryan notes in *Crippled*, her searing account of the demonisation and abuse of disabled people at the hands of austerity policies, Duncan Smith has been unashamedly explicit in his intention to target and de-legitimise disabled people's welfare rights, telling the *Daily Mail* in 2014 that "we'll root out the benefits cheats who pretend to be ill for money" (Ryan 2020: 4).

Vas's local authority had been able to do little to help, other than offer her a council property in Slough, more than 30 miles from London. Vas understandably did not want to leave her local area for fear it would disrupt her younger children's schooling and leave her alone with no emotional support from the community she has lived in for more than 20 years. Like Jane, she felt particularly perturbed by what lay implicit within the policy, that social tenants do not and should not have the same rights to home as owner-occupiers. She noted that: "I made quite a lot of changes to this place over the years to improve it. I paid for that all myself and I get nothing back. And now I'm being charged and told to move to Slough!"

Vas had lived in her house for many years and had, as is common, indeed expected, practice among homeowners, over the years made alterations and improvements, for example replacing the floors and kitchen cabinets (her partner worked in construction, and so helped to make a lot of these changes). The work of anthropologists such as Daniel Miller has been integral in examining the intrinsic role of material objects, interior design and aesthetics within the home, and the importance of such materiality in the construction of our identity, and how we make sense of the world (see, for example, Miller 2001; 2008). The home is often understood as a space through which we can assert our autonomy through material objects. However, as the geographer Kathy Burrell notes, domestic autonomy is often dictated by wider social and economic influences: that social and economic forces can *unmake* domestic space, making its perception as a space of personal freedoms something of a fallacy (Burrell 2014, see also Baxter and Brickell 2014). Therefore, unlike if they were homeowners, the repairs and refurbishment that Vas and her partner have made over the years now only highlight the lack of autonomy they ultimately have over their home. While homeowners might reap the rewards of home improvement, both in terms of aesthetic pleasure in the homespace, and financial gains as the value of their property increases, for Vas this work threatens to be lost as a consequence of her tenure status. No matter how she improves or personalises her home, Vas is left fundamentally lacking control in almost every aspect of her housing choices.

Vas's experience also embodies the relationship between housing politics, displacement and social cleansing in the capital. The bedroom tax and other housing policies, such as estate 'regeneration' and cuts to Local Housing Allowance rates,[11] that are clearly targeted at low-income and working-class communities, work to reframe London as a city that, beyond just being unaffordable for low-income Londoners, is inherently no longer *for* such communities. Austerity rhetoric has cemented an unnuanced logic regarding housing affordability in London: simply, that if you cannot afford to live in the capital, then you should leave (BBC 2010; Slater 2016b). This was certainly Vas and her partner's experience. Her connection to her home and her personal circumstances were dismissed by her local authority – she cannot afford to live in London anymore, so she should move to Slough. This in spite of the fact that moving would uproot her from her support networks, her children's school, everything she had known as home for the past two decades. Here, Vas's circumstances are dehumanised: she is seen as a problem that needs to be removed, rather than a human being with a right to make decisions about their home.

In its conception, the bedroom tax was narrativised as a pragmatic and morally justifiable policy that reduces waste in housing stock by disincentivising people to have unused rooms in their households. What is left out of these assertions of pragmatism are the integral and intimate ties that people have with their homes. Despite their increased struggles to pay rent, both Vas and Jane insisted that they would not move. As Jane made clear, the flat is her home – it is where she has lived for two decades. It is where she feels safe, with her friend and family support networks nearby: "I wouldn't consider moving, no. It's not that easy to leave behind. … Your whole ability to function depends on your housing."

The bedroom tax removes social tenants' ability to function in the everyday without fear of eviction and dispossession. Rhetoric surrounding the bedroom tax both divorces the concept of housing from understandings of home and, paradoxically, uses a moralised construction of the ideal home to dismiss and dismantle the homelives of those who do not frame their relationship with it through market logics (Madden and Marcuse 2016; Nowicki 2017, 2018). For many social tenants penalised by the bedroom tax, their homes, once secured through lifetime tenancies and affordable rents, have been placed under threat. The spectre of forced eviction and displacement as an outcome of rent arrears has become a long-term, everyday fixture in their relationship with home, creating a permanent sense of crisis. As David Madden and Peter Marcuse note in their book *In Defense of Housing*: 'For the oppressed, housing is always in crisis. … Housing crisis is a predictable, consistent outcome of a basic characteristic of capitalist spatial development: housing is not produced and distributed for the purposes of dwelling for all; it is produced and distributed as a commodity to enrich the few' (2016: 10).

The bedroom tax is the outcome of a now well-established narrative that property's primary purpose is profit-making, made all the more fervent by astronomical rises in the value of London's property market over the past several decades. Those who are understood to be financially – and therefore socially – lacking in value are dismissed as unworthy of living in the capital. This in turn proves beneficial for the wealthy, who capitalise on the displacement of working-class and low-income Londoners by investing in the properties or local areas they have been priced out of. The bedroom tax contributes to this culture of displacement in London, whereby those on low incomes living in now high-value parts of the city experience a 'displacement of attrition' – they are not immediately evicted, but remaining in their homes becomes increasingly unaffordable. This is coupled with rhetorical implications embedded within the policy that heavily suggest social tenants should not be living in expensive parts of London. Together, these factors contribute to a sociopolitical climate in which low-income Londoners are left struggling to remain in their homes, both on a dwelling and neighbourhood scale.

## Impacts on health, wellbeing and family life

Connected to this slow destruction of social tenants' rights to their homes are the ways in which the bedroom tax impacts health, wellbeing and the ability to maintain family life. An aforementioned study by Suzanne Moffatt and colleagues highlights the multifaceted impacts of the bedroom tax on wellbeing. They found that fear of potential relocation, not being able to provide healthy food for themselves or their children as a consequence of indebtedness, living in inadequately heated homes during the winter, and spiralling rent arrears all contributed to increased anxiety and stress (Moffatt et al 2016). Conversations I had with affected social tenants very much mirrored these findings. People told me that increased financial concerns either exacerbated their existing mental health issues or led to them experiencing severe stress and anxiety for the first time.

Annie saw a steep decline in her ability to meet basic needs such as food and heating once she began to lose housing income as a consequence of the bedroom tax, and her mental health deteriorated drastically. She was living alone and received little support, either financial or emotional. Annie shared the following with me:

'I was [previously] paying £173 a month in rent. When they introduced the bedroom tax I was paying £268 and at one time as I had fallen into arrears it was £280. My wages per month are on average £590, so with council tax, gas, electric etc., it doesn't leave much for food or clothes. ... Last winter I had lots of early nights because I couldn't afford to heat the house and ate lots of toast because it was all I could afford. ... I can't see a way around the situation I am in ... many people have committed suicide as they just cannot live. I understand why they have done it, this would never be an option for me but it has crossed my mind.'

Like Jane and Vas, Annie had never fallen into rent arrears prior to the bedroom tax's introduction. She had already been struggling to keep afloat, but the bedroom tax had left her in a more extreme situation. The policy dismantled her ability to feed herself, heat her home and retain her mental wellbeing. Although she denied suicidal intent, she acknowledged that the policy had in some instances driven people to this, and her own contemplation highlights the devastating severity of the policy on mental wellbeing. By threatening people's ability to afford some of the most fundamental features of a secure life – being able to pay rent and feed yourself adequately – the bedroom tax is a stark example of domicide. It is emblematic of the ways in which political rhetoric and government policy purposefully consolidate precarity into some of the most crucial aspects of everyday life.

As previously highlighted, the bedroom tax disproportionately affects disabled people (Webb 2013; Wilcox 2014; Moffatt et al 2016). The policy therefore encourages the further precaritisation of those who are already vulnerable from a public health perspective. Conversations with participants further highlighted this. For Jane, the bedroom tax has meant taking on an unaffordable extra cost in a household where both herself and her teenage daughter suffer from chronic health conditions. The room deemed 'spare' by the DWP provides important storage space for her and her daughter's medical equipment. For disabled people, space for equipment, or extra room to accommodate for conditions that may also affect partners or family members, are often vital in the establishment of a secure, safe and autonomous homespace. The bedroom tax has not only denied these rights to many people, it has actively furthered a rhetoric that suggests disabled people do not have the same social value as non-disabled people (Mitchell and Snyder 2015). The bedroom tax heavily implies that the extra space disabled people may need to live their lives in comfort and security is unimportant and wasteful. The bedroom tax is an example of disabled people being presented as existing on the margins of what is deemed to be 'normal life' (Imrie 2014). The policy, through its standardised understanding of how a home should be structured and utilised in the everyday (for example, bedrooms as spaces for couples or children to sleep in, without consideration that they might have other important uses), dismisses the needs of all those who do not fit into prescribed categories of functional domestic life

The bedroom tax also has particularly far-reaching implications for another already socially and politically vulnerable group: single parents. The bedroom tax disproportionately impacts single parents, as only the parent with primary custody is allowed to have a bedroom for their children without being penalised by the policy. Therefore, if a parent without primary custody has a bedroom for their child to stay in, they will lose housing income. This inevitably places further strain on domestic lives already fractured by relationship breakdowns. In 2015, a single father took his local authority to court over their decision that he should be eligible to pay the bedroom tax. He argued that the room deemed 'spare' was his son's when he came to stay. However, the Upper Tribunal rejected his case on the grounds that a person is only legally defined as being responsible for a child if they receive child benefit. As only one parent can be in receipt of child benefit, the father was not considered to be legally responsible for his child and therefore not exempt from the bedroom tax (Coates 2016). This dismissal of single parents' rights to a suitable home is reflective of a central narrative of the Cameron era – of 'broken families' whose failures would be resolved by the Welfare Reform Act (Wilkinson 2013). In this way, the bedroom tax frames single parents without custody as lacking legitimacy in the context of a political ideology that celebrates the nuclear family to the point of fetishisation. Single parents, through the rhetoric of Cameron's broken families agenda, are seen as failing the expectations of domestic life – particularly if they are in receipt of benefits. This, in turn, justifies the non-exemption of single parents from the bedroom tax.

The bedroom tax, then, has far-reaching implications for the health and wellbeing of some of society's most precarious and sidelined groups. This is socio-symbolic domicide writ large, dismantling people's rights to home through making explicit their diminished societal value in the eyes of the governments that are supposed to be their advocates.

## Homeownership schemes: welfare for the middle classes?

The bedroom tax has destroyed many people's ability to maintain a secure sense of home. And yet, alongside this dismantling of housing welfare for low-income and working-class people, a swathe of policies was simultaneously introduced that provide state-subsidised housing support for the middle classes.

Social housing has for many years now been politically framed as a subsidisation of rent, with market rates depicted as representing the 'true' worth of property. Such discourse has consistently played an important role in the demonisation of social tenants as economic parasites. This rhetoric was exacerbated in the Conservative government's 2015 budget, which promised to bring to an end 'subsidised rent' for social tenancy households earning over £30,000 in London (HM Treasury 2015). At the same time, Conservative (coalition and majority alike) governments have, over the past decade, consistently invested in the subsidisation of several costly homeownership schemes aimed at middle-class first-time buyers. These include shared ownership, whereby people part-own, part-rent their properties (the rented part of the property is owned by a housing association), and Help to Buy, a scheme that offers would-be homeowners struggling to put down a deposit either an equity loan or mortgage guarantee backed by government funding. Much like housing benefits and social housebuilding, such schemes provide housing support from the state that enables some people access to housing in spite of high market costs. However, subsidised homeownership schemes are framed as something different entirely, a means to climb the holy grail that is the property ladder and thus providing a path to independent living, rather than the stagnant state of dependency that social tenancy is so often portrayed as. This is in spite of the fact that homeownership subsidy schemes and social housing are clearly both forms of state-supported housing. The difference between the two lies, crucially, in who is being offered the support.

This can be considered a reappropriation of welfare that acts as something of a Robin Hood in reverse, taking welfare support from the poorest to give to those who need it far less. The almost simultaneous implementation of the bedroom tax and homeownership schemes further indicates the cavernous differences in how people are valued based on their tenure (or aspired tenure) status. Held together, the policies' parallel implementation suggests that only those who are able to aspire to neoliberal, individualist notions of ownership are deserving of state support. The bedroom tax is morally justified through its framing as a necessary means of curbing the 'wrong' kind of welfare. This once again highlights how austerity governments have defined who is deserving of home, and who is not – a moralisation of state support, rather than the pragmatic, necessary cost-cutting that has been claimed of welfare reform.

The final section of this chapter extends this point further. I argue that perhaps the most malign impact of the bedroom tax lies in how it not only perpetuates tropes of social tenants as undeserving of their homes, but encourages social tenants *themselves* to subscribe to this narrative.

## Internalising domicide

The bedroom tax has undoubtedly had a detrimental impact on affected social tenants in various ways, precaritising their homes through the threat of forced eviction and financial instability, and targeting already marginalised groups such as disabled people and single parents. However, the policy has also arguably had wider social implications by furthering the stigmatisation of social tenants in general. The bedroom tax serves as a medium through which to further instil and entrench perceptions of social tenants as undeserving and socially parasitical. Indeed, the official title of the policy, the 'removal of the spare room subsidy', evokes a sense that the government are taking back a poorly used luxury afforded to an undeserving group. The use of the word 'spare' feeds into depictions of social tenants as selfishly living in subsidised houses with rooms they do not need at the expense of the taxpayer. The policy's official name also highlights a governance strategy that seeks to mask the intimate nature of such a policy – that these are underused properties filled with spare space, rather than people's homes. Such rhetoric has worrying implications for social tenants in terms of their perceived social position.

Indeed, some participants commented on feeling a need to present themselves as 'good neighbours' due in part to the policy's effect on public perceptions of social housing. Tenants were increasingly aware that they are being 'othered', framed as enjoying untold luxuries paid for by hardworking taxpayers. Jane commented that:

'I feel like I constantly need to justify the fact that I live in a council house. I feel like I need to prove myself as a good neighbour so all the homeowners on my street will think "Oh they're [meaning social tenants] alright really" ... There's a real sense of "them and us" that I've never felt before. ... Recently I was chatting to my neighbour about improvements needed on the street, rubbish collection, street lighting, things like that. He turned to me, very amicably sounding, and said, "But it's not like you pay for it anyway, is it?" That really hit me.'

For Jane, the policy has left her with a sense that, for the first time, she must justify her position as a social tenant to her neighbours. Despite her best efforts to 'prove' herself to the homeowners on her street, Jane's neighbour continued to understand her relationship with home as less valid than his own. He assumed that she did not pay council tax as a result of her status as a social tenant, and insinuated that this meant she did not have the same claims to the street and community as himself. The jovial manner in which he commented on this, and the fact that he did so directly and without embarrassment, highlights that imaginings of social tenants as socially parasitical have become so deeply normalised in everyday public rhetoric that to voice such opinions, even to a social tenant themselves, is not to confess a hidden prejudice, but rather to speak comfortably of something perceived to be 'truth'. And while negative stereotyping of social tenants is nothing new, the bedroom tax has contributed to further cementing this rhetoric. The neighbour that so overtly stigmatised Jane had known her for decades, had always been perfectly friendly to her, and had never made such a comment before. Jane was convinced that his change in attitude (or at least the outward expression of a previously private opinion) was directly linked to the introduction of the bedroom tax. As far as she saw it, Cameron's welfare reform agenda had enabled people to justify and legitimise their class-based prejudice.

Through its language of supposed fairness, the bedroom tax has consolidated the stigmatisation of social tenants as morally justifiable. This has, in turn, left people like Jane forced to defend their tenure status in an already hostile social and political climate, whereby social tenants are framed as workshy scroungers (Tyler 2013; Welshman 2013; Crossley and Slater 2014). The pressure felt by social tenants to 'prove' that they are deserving of their homespace in the wake of the bedroom tax highlights the ways in which the policy has, for some, dislodged their sense of belonging within their own homes. The bedroom tax contributes to and extends assumptions that social tenants are taking what they have not earned at the expense of the hardworking homeowner (or aspiring homeowner). This places social tenants in the position of feeling that they must prove themselves otherwise. Through the bedroom tax, domicide is enacted through a disconnection of the home as something that all humans have the right to, instead being framed as something that people must earn. Jane's experience of the policy speaks of a rhetoric that implies that if you do not own your home, then you do not deserve to be there. The time spent making a council property home, or making friends and connections in a community, becomes meaningless in the face of policymaking that sees home through a binary lens whereby the only people that have any real claim to home are those that own property. The bedroom tax, in particular, characterises such rhetoric of the undeserving nature of the social tenant in relation to space, implying that social tenants take up too much of it when they have 'done nothing' to earn such purported luxuries as a second bedroom. The bedroom tax is, therefore, a stark reminder from the Coalition government (and the proceeding Conservative governments that have maintained the policy) that social tenants are subject to the whims of governance and political discourse that determines the type of home they are deserving of.

Since her encounter with her neighbour, Jane admitted that she now feels reticent about revealing her tenancy status to others. She remarked, "I wouldn't advertise the fact that I'm a council tenant, or that I pay the bedroom tax … I guess the way things are now … I feel ashamed". For Jane, the stigmatisation of social tenants has become entrenched to the point that she identifies with such tropes herself, feeling a sense of shame at her tenure status. Teresa Caldeira has referred to this internalisation as the 'dilemma of classification' (2001), whereby those that are socially demonised replicate the same language and rhetoric when referring to themselves and/or one another. Such self-stigmatisation also relates to the Foucauldian concept of 'technologies of the self', or self-regulation through particular governance practices. In this context, structures of governance that are enacted through intimate spaces such as the home work to promote self-classification and self-regulation, and thus self-denigration and the justification of prejudice, even among those against whom the prejudice is directed (see Foucault 1991). Self-classification is a fundamental means of social construction and control, as people who see themselves through the same stigmatising lens as others do provide unequivocal justification for their further denigration. For social tenants, the implementation of the bedroom tax provided fertile ground for a form of self-classification that sees some conforming to the very same framings imposed upon them externally by others. This inevitably further compounds their precarity and the precarity of their homes. The 'dilemma of classification' threatens to leave the trope of social tenants as workshy benefit scroungers unchallenged, and foregrounds the potential for additional domicidal policies to be implemented in the future. Therefore, by reducing social tenants to these crude, cruel depictions, the bedroom tax succeeds in entrenching an internalised acceptance of domicide. This is perhaps the most dangerous form of domicide of all – a method that encourages people to destroy their sense of home from the inside out.

The bedroom tax, therefore, establishes domicide in a variety of ways. Through a purposeful hierarchical framing of who is and is not entitled to domestic space, Cameron's government built on existing negative tropes of social tenants to frame the dismantling of their rights to home as a legitimate moral project. This reiteration of social value based on tenure type enabled them to simultaneously provide state-supported housing for owner-occupiers with little resistance, or indeed comment. Further still, the idea of social tenancy as wasteful and shameful has become entrenched even among social tenants themselves.

3

# Temporary is the new permanent: temporary accommodation policy and the rise of family homelessness

The previous two chapters explored how ideological shifts in the UK stemming from the rise of neoliberalism in the 1970s and 80s altered the country's housing landscape. Social housing, once an emblem of hopeful societal progression, became the centrepiece of revived class prejudice. The bedroom tax – the focus of Chapter 2 – is just one cog in a machine of disinvestment in and derision of social housing as a valid choice of home. Despite the underlying premise that pivoting away from social housing is part of a long-term campaign to support increased homeownership, the reality is that the mass privatisation of housing stock has instead given rise to a rapidly growing, and incredibly unregulated, private rented sector. In this chapter, I begin by examining the rise of the private rented sector and the snowball effect of family homelessness. Following this, I interrogate the increasing state emphasis on temporary accommodation – including purpose-built iterations – as a homelessness solution. With a focus on a purpose-built temporary housing scheme in Lewisham, south London, I argue that such schemes are ultimately domicidal in their further establishment of temporariness and precarity as the norm for working-class and low-income families.

## The rise of the private rented sector

As discussed in previous chapters, Margaret Thatcher's government introduced the Right to Buy scheme in 1980, stripping the UK of much of its council housing stock and flooding the housing market with privately owned homes. Alongside this, the 1980 and 1988 Housing Acts deregulated the private rented sector and introduced assured shorthold tenancies. This has meant that landlords are now able to set and raise rents to whatever they wish, and evict tenants without reason using section 21 of the 1980 Act. This almost entirely unregulated sector is now the second most common (owner-occupation, though dwindling, remains the most common), and fastest-growing, tenure in the UK (Wilson and Barton 2019). According to the Office for National Statistics (2018), the number of households living in the private rented sector in the UK rose from 2.8 million in 2007 to 4.5 million in 2017, an increase of 63 per cent. Although the typical private renter tends to be imagined as a childless twentysomething at the start of their career and awaiting their first step onto the housing ladder, the reality is that the demographics of private renters are changing. While younger households (25–34 year olds) remain the most common group of renters (35 per cent), the proportion of people aged 45 to 54 in the sector increased from 11 per cent to 16 per cent between 2007 and 2017.

One of the biggest shifts has been in the proportion of households with children living in the private rented sector. In 2007, 18 per cent of households with children were living in private rented accommodation. By 2017, this had risen to 35 per cent. This has meant a huge rise in the number of families living in a sector that has temporariness and insecurity built into its foundations. The same 2018 ONS report revealed that 62 per cent of households in the UK private rented sector had spent under three years living in the same accommodation. No caps or regulations on rent rises and the existence of section 21 notices puts tenants in an extremely precarious position, whereby the rug – both proverbial and literal – can be pulled from under them at a moment's notice. In this sense, domicide is built into private rental policy and legislation (or lack thereof), the constant spectre of eviction and the dismantling of home looming over renters. Indeed, during the ten years I spent as a private tenant in Brighton and London, I was evicted twice by landlords using section 21 notices – a story so common among my friends that it bordered on the mundane. Moving twice in one year was not an uncommon occurrence, and again treated as a normal part of being a private renter. This near-constant threat of eviction is exacerbated by consistently rising rent prices across the UK. In England for example, between October 2019 and September 2020 the median monthly rent was £725, the highest ever recorded. And in London, this almost doubles to £1,435 – rising even further to £1,690 when looking at only inner London boroughs (Office for National Statistics 2020).

Extortionate rents in the capital, of course, by no means guarantee high-quality housing, and these astronomical costs often leave people with little choice but to live in overcrowded, unsanitary and unsafe conditions. This combination of high costs, high demand and next to no regulation has created fertile ground for rising criminality in the sector. According to a recent study by researchers at Cambridge House and the University of York on what they term the 'shadow private rented sector', common criminal acts can range from scamming people out of deposits, to refusing to fix problems in a property, to practices of illegal eviction. In short, it is not hyperbole to say that it is a sector that is out of control. It is no wonder, then, that the end of a private-sector tenancy is now the leading cause of homelessness in London (Spencer et al 2020).

The unaffordability of the private rented sector has been exacerbated all the more by changes made to Local Housing Allowance (LHA) in 2012 – another component of Cameron's welfare reform. LHA is the housing benefit component for people living in the private rented sector. LHA rates vary by local authority, and are based on rent prices in that area. Prior to 2012, rates were capped at the 50th percentile of rent prices, essentially meaning that the cheapest half of the rental market was covered by LHA for people in need of income support. This was reduced to the 30th percentile as part of the Welfare Reform Act. On top of this, the Shared Accommodation Rate – a component of LHA that meant single people under 25 were only allowed to claim at a rate based on a single room in a shared property – was extended. The extension means that now single people under 35 can only claim the Shared Accommodation Rate. In London this has meant that the amount of welfare people are entitled to has at least halved in all boroughs (Wilkinson and Ortega Alcázar 2017). In their in-depth work on the impact of changes to LHA rates in the austerity era, Eleanor Wilkinson and Iliana Ortega Alcázar (2017) have highlighted how, in rhetoric very much akin to that used to justify the bedroom tax, these changes are framed as increasing fairness in the sector. The reality, they argue, is a housing system that penalises single people, and particularly those who struggle to live in shared housing for a range of reasons, from poor mental health, to childhood trauma. Once again, this policy change is emblematic of normative assumptions of home across the lifecourse – an expectation that single young people can either live with their parents or other single people during their twenties and early thirties, before entering privately owned nuclear family households in later life.

While this decimation of single people's rights to home is devastating and certainly worthy of attention, the majority of this chapter will focus on another extremely precarious group living in – and evicted from – the private rented sector: families. For those families who do not follow the assumed housing pathway to property ownership, the precarious, unregulated and unaffordable private rented sector often remains their only option, particularly in an era when social housing stock has been decimated. This extends housing discrimination into familial, as well as single life for those who do not meet the narrow expectations of home set by government narrative and policy.

The remainder of this chapter further considers some of the fallout of a private rented sector where temporariness and precarity have become a normalised condition. In particular, I focus on its impacts in terms of increases in family homelessness and local authority reliance on temporary accommodation as a supposed solution to this. I do so by drawing on interviews with eight families in Lewisham, south-east London undertaken from 2017 to 2020 who had experienced homelessness and been placed in experimental purpose-built temporary accommodation for a two-year period. The interviews were part of a project with my colleagues Katherine

Brickell and Ella Harris, hence my shift to the pronoun 'we' when referencing the research undertaken.[1]

## The rise of family homelessness and temporary accommodation

Perhaps one of the most devastating outcomes of London's increasing unaffordability – in part driven by the highly precarious and unregulated private rented sector – has been the rise in family homelessness across the capital. When we hear the word 'homelessness', the predominant image for most will likely relate to rooflessness – a rough sleeper, usually single, usually male. But over the past decade in particular, a typology of homelessness where one has temporary shelter, but no home, has risen sharply. This has especially been the case for families. In the first quarter of 2019, there were more than 88,000 children living in temporary accommodation, a 33 per cent increase since 2014 (Reynolds and Dzalto 2019). A 2019 report by the national housing charity Shelter revealed that 6,370 households with dependent children became homeless in the 2018/19 financial year. This is the equivalent of a child in London becoming homeless every 49 minutes. London boroughs account for 26 out of the top 30 highest local rates of homeless children in temporary accommodation in England (Reynolds and Dzalto 2019). While it is nothing new, and certainly predates the austerity era, there was nonetheless a significant drop in family homelessness in the latter part of the 2000s. However, this trend reversed in 2012, and family homelessness has been on the rise ever since (bar during a period of the COVID-19 pandemic, likely due to the eviction moratorium). Single mothers are the parents most likely to experience homelessness, with just over 20 per cent of homelessness applications in the UK in the 12 months preceding September 2020 being made by this group (Heath 2021).

In the vast majority of cases families are forced into homelessness as a consequence of eviction from the private rented sector. A 2017 report by the Joseph Rowntree Foundation showed that, in a record high, more than 100 families a day lost their homes in the UK in 2016 (Joseph Rowntree Foundation 2017). Due to the pandemic, an eviction moratorium was in place in England from November 2020 to May 2021, providing some respite during a particularly challenging time. However, rising unemployment in this period has contributed to an estimated 320,000 households in the private rented sector struggling with rent arrears across England and Wales (Whitehead 2021). This leaves a huge backlog of families who will likely be evicted in the coming months and years and have no choice but to register as homeless and be moved into temporary accommodation.

Temporary accommodation has become an increasingly normalised part of the housing market – a side effect of the growing significance of the private rented sector and the haemorrhaging of social housing since the 1980s. This was certainly the case for the families we interviewed, all of whom had previously been renting in the private rented sector and been made homeless by landlords either increasing rents or deciding to sell or move back into the properties. For single mum Clarissa, the pool of feasible places to move to in or nearby Lewisham was getting ever-smaller: "You go on the private market and you look at two bedrooms over £1000 [per month], and literally, I'm earning just over £1000 and I've got to feed two kids."

In line with the ONS data discussed above, our research found that the unaffordability of private rent was a particular problem for single income and single parent families like Clarissa's. Many of the families we spoke with had been forced to live in overcrowded rental properties because their incomes could not cover the cost of a place with multiple bedrooms. One parent had been living in a studio flat with their two children for four years when the landlord decided they wanted the property back. In other cases, parents had been living with other family members but were unable to stay due to overcrowding. For these families, unable to remain in the private rented sector, but in a political landscape where social housing numbers have been reduced to minuscule amounts, they had little choice but to declare themselves homeless and move into temporary accommodation.

While up until the 2010s temporary accommodation usually meant a flat or house, since 2009 there has been a steady increase in the use of bed and breakfast establishments (B&Bs) to house people experiencing homelessness. Local authorities have become increasingly reliant on them due to a simultaneous reduction in available housing and rising numbers of people presenting as homeless. For many families, this is often the beginning of months, sometimes years, of living in unsuitable accommodation, often with multiple moves from one form of temporary accommodation to another. Indeed, most of our participants had moved multiple times, often between four or five different temporary accommodations. This included being moved all across London – in the case of one resident, from Ilford to Maida Vale to Woolwich and then back to Lewisham in a period of under 18 months. Often they had stayed in properties for as little as three weeks before being moved again, and for many residents the promise of a two-year tenancy at PLACE/Ladywell – the purpose-built temporary accommodation to be discussed later in the chapter – would be their longest period of stability for some time.

The families we spoke with, unsurprisingly, often had very negative experiences of being moved to inappropriate accommodation, both in terms of property type and location. There was a pervasive sense of helplessness, of being passed from pillar to post without any say in the matter. Families who had been moved across various boroughs, often far from their jobs or children's schools, were fearful of complaining or not taking up offers, as this might result in them being moved even further afield:

'What choice do I have? Like, moving you outside London, because they've done that to loads of people.' (Jo)

'I had a choice, east London or Croydon or Birmingham.' (Ashley)

There was often frustration at Lewisham Council's definition of what constituted an appropriate location. According to one resident, the criteria was that people be within 90 minutes of places of work and school. The long and difficult commutes faced by families had a direct impact on the school lives of their children. Because families were only temporarily rehoused in the various locations they were placed in, it usually made most sense to keep their children in school in Lewisham, so as to minimise disruption to their education. However the distances to Lewisham from their temporary accommodation often made getting to school regularly and on time very difficult, especially where siblings of different ages or with varying needs were not in the same schools or nurseries. Residents described how they were: "Driving here and there and everywhere, phoning up, so sorry, they won't be in today, so sorry they're late today, just constant, but they don't put any of that into consideration" (Clarissa).

Vicky Foxcroft, MP for Lewisham Deptford described the impact on children, as she had witnessed it, of these long travel times, explaining that: "When their kids are going to school, they're literally falling to sleep because they've been awake two hours before, two hours afterwards, they're travelling, you know, when's the time to do their homework, or their extra activities, all living in a one-bedroom place."

Clarissa's experience very much chimed with this, as she recalled having to wake her primary school age children up at 5 am in order to get them up and ready to get to school on time, and the guilt and worry she felt at having to do this.

As well as being moved to inappropriate locations, the short notice period for moves between temporary accommodations was often very problematic and difficult for families. As Clarissa and Ashley explained:

'If they tell you you are moving today, they've not given you any notice, they just call you up and say by 2 o'clock you must be out of there.' (Clarissa)

'I literally got a phone call about half 8 in the evening and they said you've got to have everything out by 8 o'clock in the morning and come to pick up the keys, and we didn't know where or anything.' (Ashley)

These short notice moves were deeply unsettling, leading residents to feel like they had, in the words of Clarissa "lived my life in boxes, opening, taking back, putting things back and bringing them out, you know?". The frequency of moves made it difficult for residents to maintain jobs or provide a stable atmosphere for their children. Participants described how the moves were confusing for young children and their struggle to not let the impact on their own mental health affect their role as parents: "I'm only human, sometimes I've broken down and my daughter will find me in my bedroom asking me, 'Mummy, why you crying' and I'm thinking, 'no no I'll just pretend [everything's OK]'" (Ally).

The traumas of frequent moves were made worse by the fact that the reason for them was often not discernible for the residents: "I'm thinking, okay, I been in a two-bedroom … and you are rehousing me back in, ummm, another two-bedroom temporary accommodation. Why? You know? Why are you moving me?" (Ally).

Moving often and at short notice also had high financial costs because, without knowing where they would be and for how long, residents often had little choice but to keep belongings in expensive temporary storage costing, according to one resident, upwards of £400 a month. Another resident described paying weekly storage costs for several weeks because of uncertainty about their move dates: "They told me it was temporary for two weeks. Two weeks turned into a month, then a month turned into another, and then my things were in storage for two months" (Claire).

The cost of hiring removal vans for frequent short notice moves was also a problem for residents. Keeping money back for this was obviously difficult for families on low incomes, particularly as they usually did not receive help from the local authority with relocation costs. This dual unpredictability, of not knowing where they would be or when, and not knowing when they might suddenly need access to money for removals made it very difficult for families to plan ahead, and further compounded their precarious situations: "You try so hard to plan, but at the end of the day, they just keep telling you if you are in temporary accommodation we can't do much" (Anthony).

The temporary accommodation families were placed in was also frequently inappropriate for their needs, overcrowded and poorly maintained. One participant described to us how they had been allocated a one-bedroom property for three adults, two female and one male. The man, the uncle of the adult women, had been unable to sleep in the property with them for religious reasons. He had ended up sleeping in his car or taking night shifts at work as a consequence. Another participant explained how they and their family had been placed in accommodation that was unsuitable for a child with autism. The child was very sensitive to changes in their surroundings and needed a reasonable amount of personal space, but in this property had been required to share a room with their parent and siblings. Much of the temporary accommodation residents had been placed in also lacked basic facilities or included appliances which were too costly to run.

'When we got in there, there was nothing, not even a bed cover, not a kettle, nothing, and then we never had no heating ... they [the council] went and got us a fan heater, it just wizzed £20 on the electric, gone, in about an hour, two hours, it was mad.' (Ashley)

Frequently, properties were overcrowded. Many parents with two children had been placed in one room in bed and breakfasts for months at a time. One of our participants reported being provided with only two beds for themself and their two teenage children. Communal facilities were often overcrowded too, and it was common to have to wait long periods of time to use bathroom and kitchen facilities. Some participants also felt unsafe sharing with strangers. All participants described to us the generally poor condition of temporary accommodation. Properties were cold, damp and often infested with vermin, such as ants, mice and rats. Ashley recalled finding rat droppings which, understandably, made them scared for the health of their baby. What made these conditions worse was the perceived lack of right to complain about and fix the terrible conditions they were living with. Indeed, Ashley had lost a job because of taking the day off to go to the council and complain about the condition of their accommodation. This illustrates the difficult position families are often in – they are already at capacity in terms of the amount of time they are spending trying to sort out a tenable living situation, and the amount of stress they can deal with, as well as in many cases experiencing other forms of precarity beyond their housing status, such as job insecurity. This leaves them without the time, energy or security to push for better conditions in temporary accommodation. Participants also felt powerless to complain about these conditions because they knew that if they refused to stay in the properties they ran the risk of being deemed legally 'intentionally homeless'.[2] Joe recalled complaining about the temporary accommodation he and his family had been offered: "I phoned up and they said like ... that's your accommodation, if you don't take it you're making yourself homeless."

The rules around intentional homelessness are controversial. Numerous charities and advocacy groups have campaigned against decisions by local authorities to deem tenants intentionally homeless due to their being in rent arrears or their failure to accept relocations (Fiaz 2018; Urban 2018). People also cannot declare themselves homeless until the day of eviction, as this too will lead to rulings of intentional homelessness. Our participants were widely frustrated that this left them unable to plan anything, even when they had been given advanced eviction notices. They were also upset that the system necessitated going through the intensely stressful process of being unable to leave until the end of their notice period and then enduring the ensuing legal proceedings and bailiff visits. Ally and Clarissa both spoke of the trauma of having no choice but to wait for eviction before seeking help from the council:

'She [the council employee] said, if I was you, I would pack up your home the day before and have it, either go and put it in storage, or have it in a lorry ready. And then, that morning of the eviction, they come, cause obviously there's a procedure the landlord had to follow ... so anyway I followed procedure, which was, I thought, crazy, I packed up the day before ... and it was just ... to be honest all I did was cry.' (Ally)

'I was given notice, but these days with the council, I'm telling you, even though you're given notice, until bailiffs come to your door they won't do nothing ... they won't rehouse you until they know, okay things are outside the door and they've chained the locks on our door ... I went to the council and they're like ... are you sure the bailiffs are there?' (Clarissa)

Such experiences are devastating, but far from unique. They highlight the ways in which the absence of a secure and appropriate home can leak into so many aspects of life, particularly for young children and their parents. The above accounts are just a few of the ways in which trauma has become embedded into the housing system through the combined decimation of social housing and flourishing of an unregulated and unscrupulous private rental system. Here, domicide is enacted through a wholesale neglect of those who are unable to keep afloat in London's precarious private rental sector. Housing policies and legislation that funnel young families into overcrowded and poor-quality temporary accommodation, and leave people with no choice but to wait for the bailiffs to come before seeking help, are ones that inarguably actively destroy people's ability to establish and maintain a home for themselves and their children.

## Enter PLACE/Ladywell

'If this is the future of temporary accommodation I turn round and say well done to them.' (Ashley)

While temporary accommodation in London tends to be poor quality, insecure, inappropriately located and overcrowded, there are increasing efforts being made to improve this. Mine and my colleagues' work with homeless families began in 2016 when we were awarded a grant by my former institution[3] to evaluate new 'pop-up' temporary accommodation in Lewisham called PLACE/Ladywell. As well as interviewing eight (out of 23) households living in the scheme, we spoke with employees of Lewisham Council, the project architects Rogers Stirk Harbour + Partners (RSHP), local MPs, the show flat interior designer and the graphic design company who created PLACE/Ladywell's promotional materials.

According to its architects, PLACE/Ladywell is a "deployable residential development", built using "volumetric construction" methods. It currently occupies a site in Ladywell, Lewisham. The site was formerly home to the council-run Ladywell Leisure Centre, which was demolished in 2014. The building was designed in response to the vacant space left by the leisure centre's demolition. The site is in a prime position in Lewisham, well connected by transport and close to local amenities. Given the worsening housing crisis in the borough it was decided that the best use of the site would be for housing provision. In 2017 there were 1,800 homeless households in temporary accommodation in Lewisham, up 96 per cent since 2011 (Lewisham Poverty Commission 2017). A large percentage of these families are in nightly paid accommodation, which is very expensive for the council, and many others are living in substandard private accommodation, underscoring a need for high-quality, council-owned temporary accommodation. According to one of PLACE/Ladywell's project managers, it is more economically sustainable for the council to provide their own accommodation, rather than paying private landlords. This is because they provide what is often unsuitable and poor-quality accommodation for which they regularly knowingly charge more than the LHA will cover, ultimately requiring the local authority to top up the rents.

The development of PLACE/Ladywell from conception to its opening was a two-year process. As well as drawing on the council's housing revenue and receipts from Right to Buy sales, the project required further funding from the Council's general funds. According to PLACE/Ladywell's project manager in 2017, rental income from the flats generates £330,000 a year, which equates to a £220,000 net surplus to the Council. This means the building, which cost £5 million in total, will theoretically pay for itself in ten years. The building also exceeds the specifications of the London design guide by 10 per cent in terms of quality and size. It is clad with vibrantly coloured panels, and is very noticeable from Lewisham High Street.

PLACE/Ladywell is largely manufactured offsite and its modular components are designed to be assembled rapidly in situ. The rationale for this construction style is that the building can be moved to other sites in the future and assembled in different configurations to suit the requirements of each place (in theory anyway – more on this later). This form of 'pop-up' temporary accommodation has proven popular with local authorities, and is being taken forward by numerous councils across and beyond London, including Ealing, Bromley and Reading.

As well as alleviating immediate housing need for 23 families, a key intention of PLACE/Ladywell is that it serve as proof of concept for modular, mobile temporary accommodation as a housing crisis solution. The project manager described how "it's very difficult to have high-quality meanwhile housing", which has been a barrier to using vacant sites to meet housing need. PLACE/Ladywell solves this problem because while its occupancy of each site is temporary, the building itself was designed to be durable and last at least 60 years (Osborne and Norris 2016). This means it can theoretically be moved around the borough to utilise vacant land for housing provision where needed, without compromising on the quality of the accommodation. This 'meanwhile' use model is also valued by the council because, as the project manager describes, it allows housing to be provided quickly without having to 'scupper the future potential of the site', as could be realised with a longer planning window. These potentials, as they clarified to us would include building a larger, permanent development including "as much affordable housing as possible, by the Council, once PLACE/Ladywell moves … meanwhile use buys time to properly consider approaches, consult with residents and assemble funding". While the mobilisation of vacant sites to meet housing need raises the question of what will happen when there are few remaining council-owned sites to be sold, it enables, in the medium term, land to be found for temporary housing at a time of limited funding and policy restrictions.

Because PLACE/Ladywell is designed to be proof of concept for modular, mobile housing, it was important that it was a positive, successful example of this format in order that future developments gain political backing. The project manager describes how "[u]nderstandably, the first thing politicians think about when you say to them moveable temporary accommodation … they think shipping container shanty towns … and there was a conscious effort, I think, in designing the project, to demonstrate that this was achievable without compromising on standards."

Although PLACE/Ladywell consists of 24 flats, the housing provision was initially for 23 families, as one of the flats in PLACE/Ladywell continued to be used as a showroom. According to the project manager, almost every local authority in London had been to see, or at least expressed interest in, PLACE/Ladywell. The development had also had visits from other parts of the UK, and international delegations from America, Australia, Ireland, India and Sweden. In 2016, the building won the Mayor's Prize and the Temporary Building category at the New London Architecture Awards, which helped to feed plans for its expansion. The concept has proved so popular that in 2018 a conglomerate of London boroughs, led by Tower Hamlets, was awarded £11 million by the Greater London Authority to develop PLACE Ltd (short for Pan-London Accommodation Collaborative Enterprise). The non-profit company intends to develop modular, pop-up temporary accommodation across the capital.

PLACE/Ladywell is rented to families eligible for two-bedroom properties at a cost of £265 a week (before bills and council tax). Families were selected on the basis of considered need. Criteria included being currently housed far from Lewisham or living in unsuitable (overcrowded, poor-quality) temporary accommodation. Another factor was the cost to Lewisham Council. It was more cost-effective to provide accommodation to people considered to have a strong need to be in the borough. Additionally, priority was given either to those not in rent arrears, or people who were deemed to be trying sufficiently to pay overdue rent, in order to reward and incentivise timely rental payment. The local authority also selected families who had not been in temporary accommodation for too long, the rationale being that the longer you have already been in temporary accommodation the closer you are to being permanently rehoused.

Against the backdrop of their dire previous experiences of temporary accommodation, most participants were extremely excited about moving into PLACE/Ladywell. Many who were living or working locally had watched the development being built but had not known it was intended as temporary accommodation. Joe and Ally described how they felt on hearing they would be moving into the building:

'I was trying to find the address, and I saw this place and I was like, no, it can't be?' (Joe)

'I just jumped, I didn't know at the time it was temporary or anything, but I just, I was ecstatic, honestly, and my friend was like dancing with me, I was like oh my god! Oh my god! ... But it's not forever, it is temporary, but I am still forever grateful.' (Ally)

These reactions indicate the excitement felt at moving into what they could see was a much higher quality property than usual temporary accommodation. While the second quotation indicates disappointment at not being rehoused permanently, it also highlights a profound relief at the escape PLACE/Ladywell offered Ally from her experiences of homelessness so far.

## Life in PLACE/Ladywell

Participant experiences of PLACE/Ladywell were overwhelmingly positive. They were impressed by the size of the properties, which gave children space to run around. The bedrooms were also described as being big enough that two children could share happily. Ashley commented that the high ceilings and quality finishings made them feel "really special ... almost like little penthouses".

Most significantly, the high quality and spacious design of the flats in PLACE/Ladywell made them feel much more like a home for participants than any previous temporary accommodation. This was bolstered by their relatively long-term (two-year) contracts. While they remained in the temporary accommodation system, knowing they could stay at PLACE/ Ladywell for an extended period allowed the families we interviewed to partially relax and build a sense of home in a way they had not been able to previously.

Furthermore, some participants felt that living somewhere as nice as PLACE/Ladywell was preparing them for future permanent homes, partly by helping them to remember what stability and autonomy felt like and partly by giving them motivation to work towards a better future. As Ashley commented:

> 'Being able to live in something of this quality makes you want to earn, makes you want to be like right I want something in life ... I want a house with a garden ... a little swing and a paddling pool, have people round ... it's given us just that little taste of life ... and yeah, a bit of hope.'

However, a recurrent area of disagreement among participants was around opinions of the building's colour scheme. Some liked the bold colours while others thought the flats resembled Lego blocks. There were also divided opinions among stakeholders we interviewed regarding the benefits and drawbacks of PLACE/Ladywell's bright exterior. There was a desire on the part of Lewisham Council and the architects that the building should stand out on the high street. This was partly to celebrate the building's anticipated achievements, and partly to garner interest from politicians and other stakeholders who would then, hopefully, be convinced of its merits and inspired to commission and create more modular mobile properties. The high levels of interest in PLACE/Ladywell attest to the success of this. The bold design of the building certainly seems to have helped to garner interest and excitement. One London MP commented that "it's made a huge visual impact" and by looking different has managed to "generate debate" and draw attention to homelessness and the need for solutions. Arguably, the bright design also celebrates the building as temporary accommodation, working to dispel stigma. However, others thought conversely that the bold colours could reinforce and exacerbate stigma by drawing attention to the fact that the building was for homeless families, rather than allowing them to pass unnoticed in Lewisham. The bold design may also have contributed to a sense we found among residents of feeling like guinea pigs. In our conversations, participants expressed anxiety deriving from a suspicion that the primary purpose of the building was not to house them but to showcase the scheme to others. There seemed to be a conflict of interest between the immediate purpose of the building – to address the housing needs of the families living there – and its longer term goal of serving as a proof of concept.

## "It's not for us": anxiety and the internalisation of housing precarity

Ultimately, while PLACE/Ladywell had undoubtedly improved the lives of its residents for the time being, it had not significantly alleviated the insecurity they felt, both practically in terms of their ability to make concrete plans for the future, and in terms of their 'ontological security' – the wider feeling of security, stability and order which, according to the sociologist Anthony Giddens, is central to human happiness, and is often threatened by insecure housing tenure and an unstable connection to home (Giddens 1990). This lack of ontological security partly manifested among participants in anxieties regarding the future of the building. Participants were anxious about whether PLACE/Ladywell was going to be sold or rented privately and this made some feel out of place there. This anxiety was rooted in the fact that a flat was still being kept for use as a show home, and was attracting frequent visitors: "I think that's why they're keeping the show home open, yeah, I think as we all end up moving out of here I think they're gonna end up privately renting them. I think it'll be like that" (Ashley).

In part, this was concerning to residents because they – quite rightly – felt the show flat would be put to better use housing another family. However, the show flat also produced anxiety by making participants feel hyper-aware of their continued status as temporary residents. Many had made comments referring to the flats feeling "almost like penthouses" and being more appropriate "for bachelors". The continued existence of the show flat in this context heightened a suspicion that the building was ultimately not designed for people 'like them' (that is, low-income, working-class, often single parents) in the long term. This feeling was further exacerbated by the downstairs commercial units that form part of the development. Many residents deemed the businesses in these units to be overpriced and offering services and activities aimed at a gentrifying demographic rather than themselves, and this made it difficult for them to feel at home. They also saw the show flat and downstairs commercial units as a sign that it was an anomalous, lucky experience of good accommodation rather than indicative of their own housing futures. The sense of PLACE/Ladywell being too good to be true also manifested in a feeling that the flats were a test that would determine the quality of housing residents would be allocated in the future: "But I almost think that these are almost like a test, it's like how nice can you keep these cause they do come round and do, every six months, they come round and inspect the property" (Joe).

This kind of suspicion indicates the level of stress that residents were under and the amount of anxiety they had internalised from 'benefit scrounger' discourses which made them feel like, as with Jane in the previous chapter, they had to prove themselves as deserving of decent housing. This anxiety made them unable to relax despite the comfort provided by the flats themselves and the relatively long tenancies they had been offered.

Participants' anxiety regarding PLACE/Ladywell, and their positionality within the British class and housing system more broadly, was further highlighted through regularly expressed concerns regarding the building's external cladding. Many of our interviews with residents of PLACE/Ladywell took place just a few months after the Grenfell Tower fire. As discussed in the Introduction, the cause of the fire has been identified as the combustible cladding installed to the tower's exterior by Kensington and Chelsea Council. It has been argued by critics such as Aditya Chakrabortty and David Madden that Grenfell amounts to 'social murder' (Chakrabortty 2017; Madden 2017). This refers to the amalgamation of decades-long neglect of London's poorest residents, a horrific outcome of a system of governance that deems the lives of low-income people as lacking in economic and social value, and therefore unworthy of secure, liveable homes. Such neglect of Grenfell and its residents reveals an approach to housing that views worth of life as hierarchical: that, to draw on the work of Judith Butler, some lives are more grieveable than others (Butler 2009). Those deemed to be on a low social rung elicit limited concern regarding access to safe, secure housing. This sentiment was very much vocalised, and worried about, by our participants at PLACE/Ladywell. Almost everyone we interviewed brought up Grenfell in relation to their own safety (Harris, Nowicki and Brickell 2019). Mary described how: "When the Grenfell fire happened we saw the risk and ... we start[ed] to panic. Honestly, I had this fear that ... it's not safe here, and that week of just sleeping with my eyes [open] ... honestly."

Similarly, Emily worried that PLACE/Ladywell had panelling like Grenfell. She had gone as far as to look inside the panelling to try to gauge how similar it was. Residents remained fearful despite us pointing out that the newly erected building was unlikely not to be in keeping with fire safety standards, as the following exchange shows:

Interviewer:   I would hope, given this is meant to be the showpiece of the most famous architecture company in the world ... I would have thought they were far more careful.

Ashley:   But you think about it, all it would probably take is a resident ... to have a few drinks, decide to flick our cigarette over the side, and on the roof there, if the cigarette's lit and the wind's powerful enough it'll go into the corner, it can catch fire ... it could happen, come and look, if I show you, down here, you can see where it's flicked, it could happen, right?

73

This exchange illustrates the extent of Ashley's fear about the fire safety of PLACE/Ladywell. His rapid dismissal of our conjecture that the building is likely safe, and detailed insistence that he has found a potential site of risk, demonstrates the extent of his anxiety in the wake of Grenfell. Ashley's personal experience of the collective atmosphere of anxiety resulting from the Grenfell fire indicates his understanding of his own positionality within the housing crisis – an understanding that politicians are not looking out for him and his family because, as he puts it, "All they see is that you're benefits scum". Such stigmatising representations make Ashley deeply anxious about his family's wellbeing. The architecture of PLACE/Ladywell, too, acts as a compounding form of stigmatisation, its external cladding a material point of anxiety: a reminder for Ashley and his neighbours that they are the 'kind of people' that horrific events such as the Grenfell fire happen to.

Ashley's anxiety regarding Grenfell highlights an awareness that he and his family sit at the bottom of a social hierarchy that demarcates their lives as not having the same worth as the wealthy and politically powerful. While the collective sense of crisis and despair following Grenfell is undoubtedly widespread, it has an arguably disproportionate impact on how Ashley encountered PLACE/Ladywell. This stems from his reading of who he is and how he is valued within London's housing system. As Madden has argued, the Grenfell tragedy highlighted how: 'The chances of being subjected to these conditions are distributed unevenly. Inequality is built into the urban fabric and infrastructure, such that many working class and poor people ... are subjected to deadly risks from which the wealthy are protected' (Madden 2017).

Ashley's fear demonstrates his stark awareness of this uneven geography of value and precarity. Indeed, it later transpired that participants' fear of PLACE/Ladywell's cladding was not unfounded, and that we had in fact been incredibly naive about assurances from the local authority that the building is completely safe. At the time of writing, Lewisham Council are planning to refurbish PLACE/Ladywell after acknowledging that it does not meet fire safety standards implemented post-Grenfell. While the council may well have understood the building to be safe before these changes in safety levels, this nonetheless highlights the validity of participants' fears that they are 'the kinds of people' disasters like Grenfell happen to, and that this is emblematic of their limited societal value.

In short, despite the generally positive way in which participants responded to PLACE/Ladywell, the spectre of its temporariness, and their positionality as unvalued people, remained. Despite concerns regarding PLACE/Ladywell's cladding, almost all residents we spoke with wanted their tenancies to be made permanent. There was a frustration that, having finally been placed somewhere that was such a vast improvement to other accommodation they had experienced, they were going to be asked to leave again. As Joe lamented: "I wish they would just leave it, I wish they would just make this permanent for us."

## Temporary as the new permanent

Joe's sadness and resignation at the continued temporariness of their family's housing points to an increasingly common government response to the housing crisis – pivoting policy to focus on the construction of temporary, rather than permanent, genuinely affordable, housing. The prioritisation of purpose-built temporary accommodation over increasing social housing provision contributes to the domicidal nature of British housing policy by further instilling a sense that it is normal and unproblematic for working-class and low-income people to lack secure homes.

This is not to say that the development of temporary accommodation such as PLACE/Ladywell has been a complete failure. It has provided a lifeline for families who have suffered the traumas of eviction and appalling quality, overcrowded temporary accommodation. PLACE/Ladywell significantly improves quality of life for people while they are in temporary accommodation, and it is a good proof of concept that temporary does not have to mean living in horrendous conditions. However, it is a concept that ultimately prioritises flagship temporary housing over the provision of permanent social homes. The residents of PLACE/Ladywell are right to feel that the development is not for them – they remain a stopgap in plans to develop the site that do not include them. This is ultimately domicidal, as this continues and extends the narrative that working-class families are not prioritised as needing secure and permanent homes. Temporary accommodation becomes a normalised, even celebrated, form of housing for those deemed to be of limited societal value. Meanwhile, expanding owner-occupation for the middle classes remains a policy priority. In short, PLACE/Ladywell represents the logic of 'solutions' to the housing crisis – a logic that highlights just how deep-seated and normalised it is for working-class and low-income people to not be deemed deserving of home.

Indeed, the focus on using the PLACE/Ladywell site for temporary housing has ultimately meant that less housing, of all levels of affordability, will be built there than was originally planned. At a Lewisham Council meeting in January 2021, it was concluded by the infrastructure consulting firm Aecom that it is not financially viable to move PLACE/Ladywell after all – in large part due to the increased fire safety regulations post-Grenfell (Lewisham Mayor and Cabinet 2021). Instead, Lewisham have been advised that the most cost-effective scenario is to retain and refurbish PLACE/Ladywell and build some new housing around it on the site. This plan, approved in January 2021, effectively means that the 232 homes (81 social rent) planned for the site have been reduced to 69 (24 social rent). The revised plans also include the eviction of a nursery located by PLACE/ Ladywell. However, prior to this decision, the assumption had remained that PLACE/Ladywell was to be moved to another site in the borough, and Lewisham Council were preparing accordingly by starting the process of 'possession action' in order to 'decant' (read – evict) current PLACE/ Ladywell residents. By the time of the January decision, some had already been evicted from their flats. This means that formerly homeless families were again being forced to move when they had been told that they had two years of relative security in PLACE/Ladywell.

PLACE/Ladywell is, therefore, a failed experiment in a multitude of ways. First, its cachet as innovative 'pop-up' social housing now rings hollow as it is too costly to move. Second, its promise of higher quality temporary accommodation, while certainly the case in some respects, also fell short due to the need to retrofit and refurbish a building that is only five years old, and that did not meet safety requirements, a fact all the more concerning in the aftermath of the horrors of the Grenfell fire. Finally, the decision to pre-emptively decant families before a decision had been made about the future of PLACE/Ladywell is indicative that the lives of those who reside in London's new flagship, starchitect-designed temporary housing, remain unimportant compared to assuring the legacy of the project. This points to a deep-seated, and sadly unsurprising, truth regarding the role of purpose-built temporary accommodation policy. Not only will a focus on developing such schemes not resolve the housing crisis and restore people's access to decent and secure housing, but it may not even provide much temporary respite for families and individuals who have already suffered unbearable trauma at the hands of a cruel, defunct housing system.

## From purpose-built to the purposes of profit: temporary accommodation as big business

PLACE/Ladywell is far from the worst outcome of the growing prioritisation of temporary accommodation over permanent social housing provision. Indeed, in the catalogue of temporary housing policies, PLACE/Ladywell remains one of the more favourable, providing as it does good-sized and well-located accommodation. Perhaps one of the most devastating impacts of a wider reformulation of temporary accommodation as a housing crisis solution has been the rise of severe misuse of development loopholes by private developers and landlords. Permitted development rights (PDR) are the automatic granting of planning permission for certain kinds of buildings, which since 2013 covers the conversion of office blocks and warehouses into residential properties. As Cecil Sagoe, policy officer at Shelter, has highlighted, this loophole, when coupled with a now chronic lack of affordable housing and high rates of homelessness, has been exploited to turn homelessness and temporary accommodation into a profitable business model (Sagoe 2019). Developers are able to convert essentially any offices or warehouses into 'residential' accommodation, no matter how inappropriate or poor quality they are, and local councils have little-to-no ability to stop them from doing so. As Sagoe notes, PDR schemes are not subject to section 106[4] requirements to provide affordable housing, meaning that these sites are also haemorrhaging potential social homes. According to research conducted by Shelter, since 2015 over 10,000 potential affordable – including social – homes have been lost as a result of housing schemes coming through PDR rather than the standard planning system (Weekes 2018). Even more alarmingly, the accommodation developed through PDR is regularly scandalously cramped and poor quality – often termed 'rabbit-hutch' housing. This practice is especially pernicious in and around London where local authority demand for temporary accommodation units is extremely high. For example, Newbury House in Ilford is a former office block owned by an offshore company based in the British Virgin Islands. Offices have been converted into tiny 'apartments', some as small as 13 square metres (the equivalent to an average living room). Redbridge Council have been using the block, dubbed 'the worst new flats in Britain' by *Guardian* journalist Rupert Jones (2018) as temporary accommodation since 2017. The BBC exposed a similar case in 2019 in Harlow, Essex where homeless families, largely from London, have been crowded into tiny 'studio flats' in Terminus House, a former office block. Here, families displaced from the capital live in extremely cramped conditions – one mother described having to sleep on the sofa while her children had to 'eat, sleep and drink in their beds' due to a lack of space (Precey et al 2019). Families also spoke of high crime rates and regular fights and drug-taking among some residents, and their concerns around the impact of exposure to this on their children. Alongside this, PDR office conversions are often situated on industrial estates, further isolating families and ensuring that all aspects of their immediate surroundings are totally drained of a sense of home.

The *en masse* displacement of working-class and low-income Londoners into temporary accommodation outside the capital has become increasingly commonplace. A report in *The Guardian* in June 2021 revealed that one in four homeless Londoners living in temporary accommodation are being rehoused outside of their local area, in some cases as far as Manchester and Bradford (Hall 2021). These realities together constitute a dismantling of home that is multi-layered, whereby the trauma of eviction and initial homelessness is just the beginning, and is followed by suffering in horrendous accommodation that is often far from people's support networks, jobs and children's schools. This is a system made all the more pernicious by how profitable it is, with the private companies that own and manage such accommodation often charging local authorities hotel-level nightly rents to house families. In short, homelessness and temporary accommodation have become big business.

The impacts of life in temporary accommodation have, unsurprisingly, been worsened still further as a consequence of the coronavirus pandemic. Although an eviction moratorium provided temporary relief for some in private rented sector housing, for families already living in temporary accommodation, their precarity has been exacerbated by the virus's spread and accompanying lockdowns. In early 2021, I spoke with members of the policy and advocacy team at a health and housing charity based in Greater Manchester. They explained that their work with homeless clients had revealed the extent of the pandemic's impact, and what it means to 'stay at home' when that means staying in cramped and unsuitable accommodation. They recounted families living in B&Bs who were not allowed to play in outside areas, even during lockdowns, and children without the technology to access online learning when schools were closed. In one local authority, all state-run nurseries were closed during lockdown, while private ones remained open. Such stories reveal the extent to which low-income families' rights to home have been eroded by years of policies that devalue and moralise them as undeserving of any better.

To conclude, this chapter has highlighted an array of temporary accommodation types of varying quality (or lack thereof). Purpose-built schemes such as PLACE/Ladywell should be acknowledged for their provision of temporary respite for families who have experienced the trauma of eviction and homelessness. However, even the very best temporary accommodation schemes cannot make up for the real thing: permanent, genuinely affordable housing. Nor can it stem the tide of people being made homeless as a consequence of eviction from a private rented sector where contracts can be terminated and rents raised at whim. Further still, the promotion of temporary accommodation policies above the increased provision of social housing is ultimately a manifestation of socio-symbolic domicide – normalising, even celebrating, temporary homes as a long-term condition for working-class and low-income families.

To return to the discussion at the beginning of this chapter, ultimately the trauma experienced by an increasing number of families forced to live in temporary accommodation can be traced back to the unregulated and unscrupulous private rented sector. This, coupled with the parallel decimation of social housing, laid the groundwork for the most vulnerable people and families in London, and the UK more widely, to be exploited long before the 2008 financial crash took place. While private rental remains an insecure, precarious housing option there will continue to be chronically high levels of homelessness. This system, a system designed to prioritise private-sector profiteering far above and beyond all people's rights to secure, decent, permanent and affordable homes, is one that is unabashedly domicidal.

This is a system that destroys people's homes for the purposes of profit. Without increased availability of permanent social housing, schemes like PLACE/Ladywell can only make a temporary difference, and the increasing entrenchment of temporary housing as a permanent 'solution' to the housing crisis will undo any good that higher quality temporary accommodation schemes manage to muster. In essence, the relationship between the private rental and temporary accommodation sectors underscores the truth of the neoliberal, individualistic society that Margaret Thatcher so enthusiastically pedalled: that monetary profit is more valuable than the right to home.

# 4

# The criminalisation of home: section 144 and its impact on London's squatters

So far, we have explored policies impacting official forms of housing tenure. The focus of this chapter differs in that it addresses the impact of a 'non-tenure' of sorts – squatting and its 2012 partial illegalisation. While this may first appear to be an outlier of the book's case studies, what the criminalisation of squatting shares with the bedroom tax and the forefronting of temporary accommodation as a homelessness solution is its impact on vulnerable and low-income groups. As in the previous chapters, here we will explore how the criminalisation of squatting acts as an explicit form of domicide, legitimising the destruction of a form of homemaking which, though long maligned, has contributed much to affordable housing, subculture and even the establishment of social housing in the UK. Before examining the impact of criminalisation, the next section outlines squatting's recent history in the UK, and how section 144 came to be.

## The road to criminalisation: a brief history of squatting in the UK

The contemporary squatting movement emerged as a consequence of severe shortages of adequate housing in the aftermath of war. Squatting grew as a practice in the wake of the Second World War, most significantly in London, many parts of which had been left badly scarred by the Blitz. Lack of housing provision, particularly for returning soldiers, led to a direct action campaign that saw many homeless servicemen seizing empty properties – a movement that highlighted the failure of the 'Homes Fit for Heroes' pledge[1] of the interwar period. It has been argued that squatters during this time had a huge hand in putting pressure on the government to commit to the mass council housebuilding programme documented in Chapter 2. However, due in part to an alignment with communism at a time of increasing political tensions, and limited support from trade unions, the post-war squatting movement dwindled somewhat from 1946 onwards (Finchett-Maddock 2014; Platt 1999).

The movement re-emerged some two decades later with the formation of the London Squatters Campaign. The campaign was in part inspired by the 1966 Ken Loach television play *Cathy Come Home*, which depicts a young family's heartbreaking descent into homelessness. The play had a major impact on attitudes to housing and welfare, with the national housing and homelessness charity Shelter being established partly in response to its message. In 1968, after a screening of Loach's film, housing campaigner Ron Bailey led the London Squatters Campaign in the occupation of a luxury flat development in Wanstead, east London. The gesture had dual meaning, both highlighting the outrage that houses should sit empty while others are driven into homelessness, and encouraging people experiencing homelessness to establish a sense of autonomy and control over their lives (Bailey 1973; Platt 1999). The squatting scene in London grew throughout the 1970s, with famous cases such as Elgin Avenue in the borough of Westminster being occupied almost entirely by squatters from 1972–75 as it awaited demolition and redevelopment by the Greater London Council (Reeve 2015). Squatting was particularly prevalent during this period, aided as it was by a high concentration of empty properties, particularly in inner London. This encouraged entire squatter sub-communities to flourish, with squatters opening businesses and holding public events in these formerly empty spaces (Reeve 2015).

However, while initially supported in the media, thanks in part to a public presence carefully cultivated by Bailey and the London Squatters Campaign that attempted to reinforce squatting as a legitimate response to the housing crisis, this relationship quickly soured. As the squatting movement grew, young, single people, often with unorthodox lifestyles and anarchistic political views, rather than helpless families, became associated with the practice. This built upon longstanding categorisations of the poor as either 'deserving' or 'undeserving', in which squatting became firmly associated with the latter (Platt 1999). As Stephen Platt, housing activist and author, notes:

> It was one thing when squatting involved 'respectable', self-evidently 'deserving' cases of homeless families occupying empty council properties. ... It was quite another when the squatters were perceived to be less respectable and deserving- single people, 'outsiders', 'hippies', 'dossers' or drug takers ... particularly if they turned their attentions towards empty privately owned properties or were seen to have some sort of wider political agenda. (1999: 107)

Squatting's growing association with young, childless hedonists during the 1970s and 80s[2] saw it develop into a movement perceived entirely at odds with the socially conservative neoliberal political landscape emerging in Britain at this time. By the beginning of the 1980s, the squatting scene had begun to fade and fracture. This was due in part to the improved management of empty properties, the movement of many former squatters into council homes, as well as widespread public resentment towards those framed as hedonistic and socially frivolous (Platt 1999; Reeve 2015).

During this time, the legal framing of squatting also began to shift, with the practice re-narrativised as something that property and land owners were in need of protection from. Most notably, section 7 of the 1977 Criminal Law Act was established to provide protection from squatters. The law made trespass onto empty property a criminal offence in the following circumstances:

1. If there is a 'displaced residential occupier' (DRO) – someone who lives in a property and is excluded from said property by trespassers.
2. If there is a 'protected intended occupier' (PIO). This refers to someone who intends to occupy a property as a resident, has signed a certificate to that effect, and is prevented from doing so by trespassers.

The introduction of section 7 therefore simplified evicting squatters from residential property, as if a squatter resisted a request to leave on behalf of a DRO or PIO they could be arrested and removed without a (previously needed) court order (Finchett-Maddock 2014).

Squatters were next targeted legislatively via the 2002 Land Registration Act, which effectively curtailed their ability to obtain rights to land via adverse possession.[3] The introduction of the Act meant that an application for adverse possession can now only be considered after the land in question has been occupied by the applicant for at least ten years and an application submitted to the Land Registry (Cobb and Fox 2007). The Act decreed that if there has been no response from the registered title holder for two years after the application has been submitted, the occupant then becomes the registered title holder. The inclusion of an application to the Land Registry enables the owners of abandoned land to be alerted to its occupation, thus providing them with further opportunity to recover possession (Cobb and Fox 2007). This proved a major turning point in the relationship between squatting and the law: prioritising the protection of land and property ownership above the need for shelter or the utilisation of abandoned space. The Act also further framed squatting as a pseudo-criminal act, contributing to by then long-established perceptions of squatters as thieving social deviants (Cobb and Fox 2007). And yet, despite widespread conceptions of squatters as essentially criminal, squatting remained only a civil offence for another decade before a campaign in Coalition-era parliament led to its partial[4] criminalisation.

### Anti-squatter sentiment and the path to section 144

Although a controversial practice for many decades, squatting as a concept became more and more toxic in the run-up to its partial criminalisation in 2012. This was in spite of the fact that even prior to criminalisation, people's ability to squat had already long been hindered by existing laws. It was widely agreed among squatters that I spoke with for this research that the 1977 and 2002 legislation provide a lot of protection for property owners, and that squatting had certainly not been an easy lifestyle choice prior to section 144 (although criminalisation undoubtedly made it more difficult). Many of the squatters I interviewed seemed confused by the timing of criminalisation, when the practice had been derided, and yet remained legal, for so long. However, for others it felt very much expected. One participant, Tariq, believed that section 144 had been implemented in 2012 because "there was a high volume of 'evil squatter' stories at the time". He thought that this, in part, had enabled section 144 to be added as a last-minute amendment to the 2012 Legal Aid, Sentencing and Punishment of Offenders Act with very little public resistance (or indeed knowledge about the amendment's existence). Particularly vehement stories regarding the hedonistic and selfish activities of squatters arguably legitimised the desires of those who oppose squatting to see it further curtailed through law. These stories were particularly impactful during a time when the aftermath of the 2008 financial crash was being felt acutely across British society, including among property owners. Constructing squatters as a threat to property, an especially vulnerable asset at the time, arguably set the final groundwork for criminalisation.

One story in particular encapsulated perceptions of the practice as dangerous, abject and criminal in the run-up to its criminalisation. In 2011, a group of squatters broke into and squatted a house in north-west London. The house had recently been bought by a doctor and his heavily pregnant wife, who had been due to move in shortly before the birth of their child. After occupying the house for nearly two weeks, a court order was eventually issued against the squatters and the group disbanded. The media depiction of the incident made much of the fact that the couple were a Harley Street consultant and his pregnant wife. The squatters, on the other hand, were depicted as dangerous scam-artists (*Daily Mail* 2011a, 2011b): 'The Harley Street neurologist, whose Somali-born 35-year old wife is due to give birth today, said they had spent "thousands" to evict the squatters. In a bid to get their home back, they even offered them £500 to move out. The gang demanded more' (*Daily Mail* 2011a).

By placing emphasis on both the professional status of the consultant, and his partner's pregnancy, the couple were positioned within the story as ideal (re)productive members of society working hard and buying a home to raise their future family. Conversely, the description of the squatters as 'gang-like' thieves speaks to depictions of the 'underclass' discussed in previous chapters – an abject, workshy group scrounging off the hardworking taxpayer. However, this depiction of the squatter crew[5] in question is particularly malign. Unlike the lazy scrounger trope so often applied to social tenants, squatters are often depicted using language that pertains to active criminality, rather than passive worklessness. The use of the word 'gang' in this news story denotes danger and lawlessness, while 'demanded' implies the expectation of being awarded something not earned. Even when reporters acknowledged that on hearing they were squatting the home of a pregnant woman, the group apologised to the couple and cleaned the house before leaving, depictions of the squatters as callous and hedonistic remained. For example, in an article by the *Evening Standard*, after describing how the squatters had vowed to clean the house, and could be heard vacuuming before leaving, the reporter concluded with the following comment: 'The squatters left a crushed beer can in the living room of the unfurnished Edwardian house' (*Evening Standard* 2011).

The focus on the crushed beer can is emblematic of the ongoing construction of the squatter as hedonistic and irresponsible, the antithesis of the property-owning, respectable citizen (Platt 1999). The image of the distorted beer can on the floor of an Edwardian Hampstead home personifies narratives of an underclass that defaces societal ideals with selfish and lazy behaviours. Arguably, stories such as these helped to set the scene for finally criminalising the practice.

In 2010, vehement anti-squatter Mike Weatherley was elected as the Conservative MP for Hove and Portslade. Almost immediately he began applying parliamentary pressure to criminalise the practice. He tabled an early day motion[6] in 2011, and gave an impassioned anti-squatter speech in parliament in the same year, stating:

'I wish to dispel the myth once and for all that squatters and homeless people are one and the same ... squatters do not fit the profile of the kind [of] vulnerable people we should be looking out for. ... They run rings around the law. And what these professional squatters lack in respect for other people's property, they make up for in guile and tenacity. They are organised and frequently menacing. ... Members of the public are getting tired of hearing that squatters are getting so much for free when they are struggling to get by.' (Weatherley 2011a)

By dismissing any link between squatting and vulnerability as 'myth' and portraying squatters as guileful, hedonistic property thieves, Weatherley's campaign worked hard to further detach understandings of squatting from the need for home and shelter. His reference to squatters' 'guile and tenacity' sought to frame them as dangerous criminals capable of well-planned enactments of home-theft. This again highlights how squatters were constructed in political and media rhetoric as inherently criminal, providing further moral justification for the introduction of section 144.

Weatherley's anti-squatting activism gained traction in parliament, and the criminalisation of squatting began to appear increasingly likely. Homelessness and housing charities expressed concern regarding the potential impacts. The national homelessness charity Crisis published a report shortly after Weatherley's speech that countered the MP's argument, stating that squatting is in fact a common response to homelessness, rather than a guileful act of vandalism. The report emphasised that 40 per cent of single homeless people squat, and that its criminalisation would therefore result in the penalisation of an already highly vulnerable homeless population (Reeve 2011). The campaign group Squatter's Action for Secure Homes (SQUASH) published a parliamentary briefing urging MPs to reconsider the proposed illegalisation of squatting. They argued that the law change would impact adversely on already vulnerable groups, empower unscrupulous landlords and encourage property speculation, thus furthering the issue of empty properties – already a huge problem in London. They also cautioned that criminalisation would burden the justice system, police force and thus ultimately the taxpayer via court and imprisonment costs (SQUASH 2011). Despite these concerns, Weatherley's campaign gained momentum and, following a brief consultation, section 144 was added as a last-minute amendment to the Legal Aid, Sentencing and Punishment of Offenders Act 2012. As of 1 September 2012, squatting in residential buildings is illegal. A person convicted under section 144 is now liable for six months' imprisonment, a level 5 fine (£5,000), or both (Ministry of Justice 2012).

The Ministry of Justice framed the implementation of section 144 as a legislative decision providing increased protection for residential property owners via the removal of so-called 'squatters' rights'. As previously discussed, these purported rights were already extremely limited as a consequence of existing legislation. The presumed impact of section 144 was therefore that it would become 'more difficult for trespassers to assert they have rights in respect of residential buildings because their occupation of the building will be a criminal act' (Ministry of Justice 2012). Perhaps predictably, the voices of squatters themselves remained missing from the vast majority of debate around the law change. The remainder of this chapter therefore unpacks the core impacts of criminalisation, as told by squatters themselves.

## Eviction as the new normal

Section 144, as a change in law that ensures the physical removal, and potential fining and imprisonment, of squatters, enacts domicide in a multitude of ways. At its most literal, section 144 has brought about the destruction of home through increased forced eviction. While squatting has always had a longstanding relationship with forced eviction, prior to criminalisation squatters nonetheless possessed some negotiating power, particularly in terms of their ability to remain in properties for relatively long periods of time. Its dismantling via section 144 has therefore derailed an important homemaking option for low-income and other vulnerable groups.

Long-term squats have become somewhat obsolete in the post-section 144 landscape, with forced eviction an ever-present reality. The vast majority of squatters I met during my research were under continual threat of forced eviction, whether they were living in residential or commercial properties. When I met Rhys in early 2015, he told me that he had recently given up on squatting altogether, as section 144 had made it too difficult to sustain. He told me that since the law's implementation, he and his crew had avoided squatting residential properties, instead occupying empty commercial buildings (now a common practice among London's squatting community). However, these properties were also difficult to maintain for any real period of time, with local authorities and property owners swiftly issuing eviction notices once they realised a building was being squatted. Post-section 144, Rhys had lived in four or five squats over the course of a few months, with the average time spent in each being just a few weeks. Unsurprisingly, after this spate of forced evictions he decided to give up. Rhys relocated to Cambridgeshire to live with friends, his inability to establish any form of housing security in London driving him out of the hugely expensive capital. Experiencing forced eviction on such a regular basis made it impossible for Rhys to forge any long-term connection or sense of home, with every opportunity to occupy a property almost immediately disbanded. Rhys's story was a common one – multiple participants recounted being forcibly evicted from their squats with alarming regularity. Dave told me that he and his crew had been evicted from five buildings in the space of a month. While they eventually found a longer term squat,[7] the constant fear of eviction and the practicalities of finding enough buildings appropriate to squat had inevitably led to some of his friends abandoning the practice. Indeed, at a conference on the future of squatting that I attended in the autumn of 2014, a volunteer at the Advisory Service for Squatters (ASS) commented to me that the organisation's phone helpline had been "deafeningly silent" since section 144 had arrived. He lamented that people were too afraid of the prospect of imprisonment and heavy fines to continue squatting in residential buildings.

This process of repeated forced eviction is an enactment of violence embedded in squatters' everyday lives that vastly decreases their ability to secure a home, even in the short term. For Rhys and Dave, forced eviction was not an acute moment of housing precarity, but rather a constant incursion into their everyday lives. Forced eviction via section 144, then, is an intrinsic tool of domicide – the literal removal of people from places they are trying to establish as homes – and the signalling of property and land ownership as a priority above the right to home and shelter.

## Making home in the face of forced eviction: Grow Heathrow

Clearly, then, forced eviction practices have had a steadfastly negative impact on the ability of squatters to both secure and maintain a homespace in London. And yet, one high-profile squat remained standing for over a decade post-section 144. On the edge of the city, a large squat sat on disused land close to Heathrow Airport from 2010 to 2021, aeons in the context of contemporary squatting. As section 144 decimated the practice of squatting throughout London, Grow Heathrow remained, surviving numerous court battles and eviction attempts. Set up in 2010 by the climate change activist group Transition Heathrow, Grow Heathrow was established on an abandoned site in Sipson, one of the residential areas under threat of demolition to make way for Heathrow's third runway. Transition Heathrow claimed to have cleared 30 tonnes of rubbish when they first arrived on the site, which had become infamous for drinking and drug-use, attacks on young people, and other antisocial behaviour.

I arrived for my visit to Grow Heathrow on a beautiful July afternoon to a site buzzing with people – some residents of the squat, others staying for a short period, others day visitors like me. Lily, a relatively new resident, proceeded to show me around. Every structure and building had been constructed by the squatters, from the allotments that grew the vast majority of the food (this was accompanied by regular 'skipping' – taking unused food from supermarket bins), to the communal and living areas. Buildings tended to be made from wood and corrugated iron, but Lily was particularly keen to show me a building in a peaceful corner of the site made almost entirely of straw bale (along with sand and horse manure). She explained that this was her favourite place on the site, and that she and other residents often used this building to rest, write and retreat from the at times hectic nature of communal living. She showed me around the communal living areas and introduced me to other residents. A handmade, somewhat ramshackle greenhouse led to the Grow Heathrow kitchen, an open plan wooden building decorated with an array of mismatching rugs, armchairs and cabinets. This appeared very much to be the centre of activity, with a constant throng of people wandering in and out, cooking, playing guitars in the corner, or relaxing with a beer out in the greenhouse.

Despite its unconventional setting and 'make-do' aesthetic, Grow Heathrow in many ways encompassed traditional conceptions of the 'homey' home (Blunt and Dowling 2006). In his 1988 work *Home: A Short History of an Idea*, the urbanist and architect Witold Rybczynski outlined the importance of comfort in the establishment of the modern home. While Rybczynski's conceptualisation of the home was romantic and uncritical, it nonetheless highlighted the importance of comfort as a practice of homemaking – of transforming a dwelling into a home (Rybczynski 1988). It was evident that the residents of Grow Heathrow, too, sought comfort, both material and imaginative, in their home. Soft furnishings, low lighting in the kitchen/ living room area, and private rooms and buildings for sleeping and spending time alone produced a somewhat surprising sense of traditional homeliness in an anything but conformist setting. Decorations for the communal areas had been added over the years by residents past and present, and newer buildings, such as the straw bale house, were added to accommodate the expanding number of residents. The pride Lily exhibited when showing me the creative ways in which the collective had developed the site brought to mind the traditional adage 'an Englishman's home is his castle'. In spite of the precarity of life in a squat, a long-term home had been lovingly built, personalised and expanded. For Lily and the other residents, some of whom had lived on the site since its establishment in 2010, Grow Heathrow represented not only a desire for autonomy and environmentally sustainable living, but a site of comfort and identity expression through material culture, perhaps some of the most fundamental traditional aspects of a home (Miller 2001).

Grow Heathrow also disrupts sociopolitical imaginings of the modern squat as a site of immorality, hedonism and disregard for property ownership. Rather, the site clearly connected the practice of squatting to that of homemaking and community. As Lily commented, "It's changed people's ideas of what a squatter is, especially in the local area". Lily and the other residents I spoke with prided themselves on their positive relationship with locals. Grow Heathrow often held open days, events and workshops at the site, regularly attended by the wider community. Although originally established as a political response to Heathrow's proposed third runway, the squat extended beyond its original purpose as a site of protest to become a bona fide part of the local community, and a place to call home for many. Grow Heathrow therefore demonstrates that squats, although certainly often sites of subcultural and politically motivated lifestyles, are also in some ways imbued with many of the same imaginaries and understandings of the traditional British home. This is very much at odds with Mike Weatherley's depiction of squatters as guileful criminals.

Despite its relative longevity, Grow Heathrow was not immune to the spectre of forced eviction and the broader dismantling of squatting as a homemaking practice. Grow Heathrow was under threat of eviction more or less since its founding. Those living on the site faced numerous court hearings, including in the High Court and Court of Appeal, who both ruled they should leave the site (BBC 2013). On several occasions the group had to prepare for the rumoured arrival of bailiffs and, in 2017, the High Court granted a possession order to the landlords of the site, giving the Grow Heathrow residents 14 days to leave. The battle to save Grow Heathrow waged on, with the group's lawyers arguing that the residents had a right to home under Article 8 of the Human Rights Act 1988, and therefore should be allowed to continue to live on the site. However, the Court ruled that this did not overrule Article 1 of the same Act, that asserts the right of property possession (Laville 2017). In February 2019, the bailiffs finally moved in and evicted half of the site, and the remainder was evicted in March 2021.

The decision of the Hight Court and eviction of Grow Heathrow is the legal enactment of domicide – that the home as a site of shelter, belonging and comfort is understood as having inferior importance to legal ownership. Through the court system, a group were stripped from the alternative and inclusive home they had lovingly created over the past decade. For modern squatters then, the trauma of eviction is an almost inevitable outcome of their homemaking practices.

## Forced eviction and securitisation

Lily had come to Grow Heathrow because she was struggling to maintain a life in the London squatting scene. Squatting had come to consist of a cycle of procuring a squat, setting up a home, followed almost immediately by forced eviction. She felt that Grow Heathrow was a relatively secure option in comparison to what she had been experiencing. However, several months after I had first visited her at the site, Lily told me that she had moved back to the city because she had found work, although she was once again back in the cycle of regular eviction from squatted properties. She was unsure of her next move, no longer wanting to live at Grow Heathrow because its distance from the city centre made it difficult to sustain work, but equally struggling to maintain a home further into London. She felt trapped in a situation where all outcomes were precarious – she either moved back to Grow Heathrow with its limited work options, or attempted to remain squatting in the inner city, where at least she had more employment opportunities.

Deciding to stay squatting in inner London, Lily described it as "more stressful, with more risk involved". Fear of arrest has deterred many from attempting to squat residential properties. Even when squatting in commercial properties, crews are forced to move from building to building with increasing regularity. Lily also told me that she found it increasingly difficult to find viable empty properties at all, be they residential or commercial, as she noticed more technological and physical security installed in empty buildings than ever before. Harry echoed a similar experience of high levels of property securitisation making it difficult to open and maintain squats. Shortly after section 144 was implemented, he was evicted from a squat in an abandoned former north London pub. Once he and his crew had been evicted, the property owners hired nightly security guards in order to ensure it was not squatted again. Harry was appalled by this turn of events, and attributed it in part to section 144 reducing tolerance for squats in commercial, as well as residential, properties.[8] Harry had been part of a large crew that had managed to remain in the pub for several months – unusual in the post-section 144 landscape. He told me that local estate agents had in fact agreed to let them into the building if they promised to look after it and keep it secure, as they feared if left empty it would be vulnerable to vandalism. The crew became quite well known, tolerated and even celebrated among a local community that had lamented their local pub's closure. Harry and his crew were excited to take on the project, opening the building up as a social centre, hosting events and workshops, and establishing a free library and clothing 'swap shop'. He referred to the atmosphere in the squatted pub as "a community space, very social, with people just popping in". Harry felt that the crew's community focus had made them popular with many locals. Despite this local support, the building owners had them evicted, replacing them with the costly security guards to ensure that the building remained empty. Harry recounted that the eviction process had been violent and emotionally overwhelming, with bailiffs and police appearing one afternoon on short notice, giving them little time to prepare themselves to leave, and forcibly removing them from the building.

This increased private securitisation and regularity of evictions can be seen as directly related to the ever-increasing value placed on the property market in London, and the ongoing philosophy of privatisation and individualisation that the financialisation of housing drives. Section 144 is, in essence, a piece of housing legislation borne out of the fetishisation of property as commodity. As Lily remarked, "There is no public land anymore, everything has to be someone's private space". Both Harry and Lily saw their experiences of forced eviction as intrinsically bound up in understandings of housing-as-equity, as opposed to housing-as-home. Indeed, the pub Harry had squatted became a property guardianship shortly after his eviction (the commercialisation of squatting through property guardianship will be discussed later in this chapter). It has now been re-opened as a gastro and craft beer pub in an area that, like so much of the capital, has seen rapid gentrification and sky-rocketing property values in recent years. When we met again in 2016, Harry, like several of my participants, confessed that he had given up on squatting, as it had become too difficult to keep going.

For Lily and Harry, like so many other squatters since 2012, forced eviction became enmeshed within the everyday, a continual cycle of homemaking followed by home destruction. Their experiences highlight that forced eviction is not always an acute moment of emergency. Rather, in the context of squatting it has become an almost normalised element of squatters' relationships with home. They have found themselves at the sharp end of embedded conceptions of what a home should, and equally should not, be, thereby leaving them vulnerable to continual, and politically and legally legitimised, displacement and dispossession (Brickell et al 2017). In this way, the continued forced removal of squatters from their homes goes on unchallenged.

## Section 144, mental health and wellbeing

Another significant impact of section 144 has been on the mental health and wellbeing of squatters. Conversations with participants found clear connections between squatting's criminalisation and mental health deterioration. One participant, Tariq, candidly discussed with me the relationship between his mental health and squatting, and the impact that section 144 had had on his wellbeing.

I met Tariq through a friend of a friend. He invited me round to his squat, a disused former pub in south London.[9] After a cup of tea and some biscuits (a nationwide ritual of welcome in all British homes, squat or otherwise), Tariq recalled how he had come to squatting. He told me that he has always suffered from social anxiety, but that this reached its peak when he went to university, where he found himself struggling in a way he hadn't felt before: "I found I couldn't do what most people can, getting up, working a nine-to-five. ... I did a degree and found turning up to even 25 per cent of my lectures a challenge. I felt alienated from pretty much everything. ... Mental health issues I guess"

After deciding that he could no longer continue with his degree, Tariq moved in with some friends who were squatting in London while he considered his next move. This turned into several years of squatting in the capital. He credits squatting as having a hugely positive impact on his mental health, providing him with a sense of both freedom and responsibility that he had struggled to find during his time at university. Tariq found a sense of autonomy and empowerment that he had never previously experienced, thriving in the strong sense of community embedded in squatter crews and enjoying living in a physically and mentally stimulating environment. Squatting requires a strong practical knowledge base, such as electric work, welding and building repairs, as well as resourcefulness in terms of being able to live on little-to-no money. Tariq found this at times challenging lifestyle satisfying, giving him a sense of purpose that he had never felt before. As he commented, "There's something exciting about the challenge of living for free". For Tariq, having to put so much work into his home gave his life meaning and richness.

However, this sense of autonomy and control has been vastly eroded by section 144. Tariq's friend and fellow crew member, Dave, lamented that during one particularly bad month they had 'lost' five buildings shortly after entering and securing them. This was due to section 144, with Interim Possession Orders (IPOs) being issued at a faster rate in squatted commercial properties since the law change. He felt that this put a lot of strain on crews, and that squatting had become a far more stressful practice than it used to be. Tariq found that, while he had found squatting to be an antidote to his anxiety and struggles with a normative nine-to-five existence, the introduction of section 144 had drastically reversed this. Squatting in the post-section 144 landscape had increased his anxiety levels, and he worried about the uncertain future laid out before him.

Tariq and his crewmates also acknowledged the changing dynamics in larger crews that have tended to form in the wake of section 144. This is due to commercial properties, now the mainstay for squatters, needing larger groups of people to occupy and manage them successfully. Larger crews, in turn, need high levels of organisation. Where there are lots of strong characters and opinions about how squats should be run, tensions invariably arise. Tariq noted that squats had become more threatening places for women in particular. Dave added that there has certainly always been a gendered dimension to squatting, with it generally understood to be a male-dominated practice: "There's lots of sexism present in squatting. Squatting lends itself to machismo. Criminality, breaking things, using manual skills. It's 'macho glamour'." However, they felt they had seen a particular rise in sexist behaviour after section 144's implementation, with larger crews at times contributing to women feeling unsafe. They told me about a nearby squat a female friend had been living in a few months previously. In a group meeting she brought up that she felt unsafe in the squat due to some (male) crew members bringing back strangers at night. She was told that if she could not handle living there, then she should move. Tariq and Dave understood the event to be in part a consequence of section 144, as smaller squats are now nearly impossible to establish or join, therefore leaving women in particular exposed to potentially threatening situations and behaviours. Lily told me a similar story of a squat she had recently lived in, where she and her fellow female crew mates had raised the issue of misogyny in the group, only for their experiences and opinions to be dismissed by many in the (predominantly male) crew. These accounts certainly fit with a relationship between women and precarious housing that sees them regularly more vulnerable in contexts such as homeless shelters and rough sleeping, where they are often under increased threat from physical, verbal and sexual violence (Radley et al 2006). Therefore, the forcing together of large groups who may not know each other well, rather than smaller, more select squatting crews, has arguably furthered a reduction in safety and wellbeing within squats for women and other vulnerable groups.

There have, however, been clear attempts by some squatting communities to combat patriarchal tendencies in squatting culture. One collective, known as House of Brag, opened the London Queer Social Centre (LQSC) in an abandoned commercial property in Brixton in summer 2014. The aim was to establish a queer safe space for the squatting community. As their mission statement declared:

> The London Queer Social Centre is a squatted, volunteer-run, non-commercial project intended to provide a large free-to-use space available to queer/activist/liberation/radical and local communities to organise, network, share ideas, relax and have fun. We prioritise providing a space and a platform to voices that otherwise have difficulty being heard. (House of Brag 2014)

During its short lifespan, the LQSC ran a variety of workshops and events, ranging from squatting skills, yoga, sex and feminism discussion groups, and queer film screenings. When I visited the squat one evening, a group discussion was taking place about how to better protect women and LGBTQI+ squatters from the culture of machismo that exists within the practice. There were certainly no simple answers, but those involved in the discussion were clearly conscious of the prevalence of some of these issues within squatting culture, and how this had, in part, been exacerbated by the need for larger crews in the post-section 144 era. Although crews are taking steps to combat these issues, they are also inherently hindered by the fact that squatting has become much more transient in the wake of section 144. The LQSC, while an important safe space for those marginalised by elements of squatting culture, ultimately only ran for two weeks before the collective was evicted. This is an extremely short period of time within which to provide a productive voice for vulnerable members of the squatting community. While prior to section 144 squats, both residential and commercial, were more likely to be regularly established for months or years at a time, the law change has removed the opportunity to create alternative squatted spaces for any significant period. This is particularly damaging for groups such as women and the LGBTQI+ community, whose access to safe spaces is already limited.

Section 144 therefore dismantles home through impacting wellbeing. The law change dismantles the homemaking capacities of those who are already living with mental health issues, and vulnerable or under-represented groups. Displacement, therefore, becomes not just about material loss at a particular moment in time. It becomes embedded as an ongoing condition of squatting as a practice, with squatters left socially and culturally, as well as physically, drifting and placeless as a consequence of section 144. This is what David Delaney refers to as the culmination of experiential–material displacement and discursive displacement. This amalgamation of momentary and embedded displacements compounds forced eviction and home loss as inevitable for particular groups of people such as squatters – displacing them not only from their homes, but from society more widely (Delaney 2004). This is a particularly cruel incarnation of domicide, whereby those already living precarious lives are most likely to see the destruction of their homes and homemaking capacities. Perhaps more damaging still, the implementation of such policies furthers a sociopolitical discourse that such forms of domicide are a social and political necessity, further normalising the precaritisation of those that are most vulnerable.

## The 'good squatter'

As highlighted so far, section 144 is a clear example of domicide. The law change is an intentional decimation of squatting as a homemaking practice via forced eviction, and instils instability and a lack of autonomy into the everyday lifeworlds of squatters. What is also integral to the functioning of section 144 as a domicidal policy, however, are the ways in which it further frames squatters as abject. Domicide in this instance can be understood beyond solely the destruction of or the removal from the physical home, to include the ways in which marginalised groups are excluded from the right to home entirely. The remainder of this chapter considers these social, political and cultural manifestations of home destruction present within section 144.

A key function of section 144 is how it legally structures a criminal/ victim binary. The criminalisation of squatting legally frames longstanding assumptions around squatting as the tactical avoidance of social contribution, a form of theft in which hedonistic, abject figures take advantage of the financial rewards hard-earned by their victims, responsible property owners. Although these imaginaries of squatters are far from new, they have been exacerbated through section 144 via its restructuring the figure of the squatter as criminal through a legal, as well as sociopolitical, lens. As an acquaintance commented when I described my research to them, "Well they must've made it illegal for a reason".

This is complicated further by the existence of opposing, positive depictions that frame squatters as socially and environmentally conscious activists, which feeds into a 'good vs. bad squatter' binary. In public, political, and indeed academic, rhetoric, squatting is often understood as either a product of hedonism and antisocial behaviour, or it is framed as a political movement. In this vein, the sociologist Hans Pruijt outlined a framework of urban squatting, defining four squatting typologies: deprivation-based, entrepreneurial (setting up an establishment such as a social centre with little resources and the avoidance of bureaucracy), conventional squatting (squatting to protect the cityscape from redevelopment), and political squatting (Pruijt 2013). These categories understand the decision-making processes behind squatting to be based either on a lack of alternative housing options, or the desire to oppose a city's political structures.

Pruijt's typologies are certainly commonplace within London's squatting scene, with the majority of my participants practising squatting for one of the reasons outlined, at least in part. However, we should nonetheless be careful in defining squatters solely through such frameworks that often centre on the justification of squatting as a necessary and/or politically noble practice. I argue that the very process of justifying squatting establishes an understanding that squatting as a practice *needs to be justified*, that it cannot be understood simply as another form of homemaking in the city. This habitual categorisation of squatters that defines them as either societally abject hedonists or political activists draws parallels with the ways in which the poor more generally are categorised as either deserving or undeserving. This is a long-familiar trope in British depictions of the poor and working class, whereby those on low or no incomes are understood in binary terms as either workshy scroungers or infantilised, helpless victims of their circumstance (Welshman 2013). Such binary portrayals are dangerously reductive. For squatters, depictions of 'good' and 'bad' squatters constitutes domicide in two ways. In relation to 'bad' squatters, section 144 is positioned as a justified response to a degenerate lifestyle. For 'good' squatters, their squats are understood as sites of political action or urban preservation, but not as homes. Whereas the middle classes, and homeowners in particular, are rarely, if ever, forced to justify the existence of their homes, 'bad' squatters are dismissed as undeserving of home, and 'good' squatters are constantly required to justify their housing circumstances beyond the basic desire for home.

This can at times lead to resentment and social fatigue on the part of the squatter. Particularly in the post-section 144 landscape, squatters are often left feeling further obliged to prove their status as 'good' in order to justify their existence and keep their homes. This further entrenches binary understandings of the subculture. Some of the squatters interviewed as part of this research commented that they resented continuously having to prove themselves as 'good' squatters that were not seeking to take advantage of or dupe landlords into lengthy court battles. Roberta felt particularly perturbed by this constant demand for self-justification, as she felt her actions as a squatter should ultimately not be of anyone else's concern. As she remarked, "All I'm guilty of is using an abandoned building in a ridiculously expensive city, where affordable housing doesn't really exist". Roberta felt that section 144 had created something of a backlash whereby some squatters, angered by a sense of legal persecution, were rejecting calls to prove themselves as responsible or community-facing. She referred to this as a "fuck you" mentality: "a lot of people are pissed off. Why should we be out there having to 'prove ourselves'?". When we met, Roberta had recently stopped squatting, as she felt that it was ultimately too tiring and life-consuming in the aftermath of section 144 to continue. Part of this was exhaustion at having to constantly justify her decision to squat.

For some participants, the act of having to prove oneself as a 'good' squatter became particularly frustrating post-section 144. Grace had been squatting in London for several years, and, unsurprisingly, was finding it increasingly difficult to find and maintain a viable home since the implementation of section 144. When we met, Grace was studying for a Master's degree, and squatting provided a means of surviving in the city on very little income. However, constantly moving from place to place had inevitably impacted her studies. She described cycling round London for days on end, hunting for new empty properties to occupy, often to no avail. She was relieved, then, when she and a group of friends found an abandoned former postal sorting office in south London. Grace decided that the best tactic for securing the building for as long as possible would be to contact its owner and try to negotiate a temporary agreement with them (an increasingly common tactic among squatters). The landlady was open to making a deal with Grace and her friends, agreeing to allow them to remain in the property over the coming winter for around three months, as long as they looked after the building, and promised not to contest the eviction notice once it had been issued (the squat, being a commercial property, was not subject to section 144).

Although grateful that she had somewhere to stay over the next few months that would allow her to concentrate on her degree, Grace also felt somewhat resentful that she had to make such promises and negotiate deals in the first place. It irritated her that she was having to work to appease people who were leaving buildings empty at a time of housing crisis. Grace commented that she also felt pressure from local residents to adhere to certain figurations of the 'good' squatter. Local residents were generally supportive of Grace and her crewmates living in the property, as it is a building that holds historic significance. Locals had been campaigning to put an end to the landlady's plans to demolish and regenerate the sorting office into high-end private housing. Grace told me that a local group leading the campaign to save the building from demolition assumed that her crew were also committed to preserving it, and wrote to them requesting their involvement with the campaign. She noted, somewhat bemused, that: "They wanted us to write a manifesto stating why we want the building to be saved … [but] this isn't about the building … it's about me having a home, having a roof over my head."

The assumptions made by locals that Grace and her crew were squatting to protect the building's heritage, although well-intentioned, inadvertently contributed to a rhetoric that detaches squatting from homemaking practices, and threatened to mask the precariousness entrenched in Grace's everyday life. Rather than acknowledge Grace and her crewmates' need for a home, the campaign group were instead focused on the architectural precarity of the building. For Grace, squatting is not predominantly a political statement, but a decision made as a consequence of limited housing options in London. A struggling student with little financial means or family support, Grace saw squatting as one of the few viable solutions to the capital's spiralling unaffordability – a solution vastly reduced by the implementation of section

144. The 'good' squatter trope acted as a point of further pressure for Grace as she tried to maintain her life in London.

The squat I visited that fell most clearly into the 'good squat' trope was undoubtedly Grow Heathrow. For the majority of its existence, Grow Heathrow and its collective of residents were portrayed as the epitome of best practice. When we discussed why Grow Heathrow was seen in such a good light compared to most other squats in and around London, Lily felt its comparative long-termism contributed in large part to its popularity with local people, who generally saw the site as a community asset. Indeed, the Grow Heathrow collective often held gardening days, school trips and for the most part were open to the public. Its image was also aided by unusually flattering press coverage from both the left- and right-wing press (see, for example, Dangerfield 2012; Williams 2013).

The nature of this particular squat appeals to depictions of the good squatter as environmentally conscious, restorative rather than destructive, and connected to the wider community – the figuration of squatting termed 'conservational squatting' in Pruijt's framework (2013). The goal of the conservational squatter according to Pruijt 'involves squatting as a tactic used in the preservation of a cityscape or landscape' (Pruijt 2013: 34). The principle behind the Grow Heathrow squat was clearly linked to the restoration and preservation of the site, as well as focusing on raising awareness of climate change and the negative environmental contribution of a potential third runway at Heathrow Airport. In the press, the collective tended to be defined in relation to their commitment to reducing carbon emissions and contributing to urban farming and gardening, often being positioned as 'green-fingered' squatters (Dangerfield 2012; Williams 2013). Lily and other residents felt confident that this somewhat unique portrayal of squatting was hugely positive for Grow Heathrow, and had contributed to its relative longevity. This should not be undervalued and ignored – clearly, acquiring the good squatter mantle can be beneficial for increasing squatters' security. However, it must also be acknowledged that, as with Grace and the former postal sorting office, there remains a concern that such narratives continue to sideline understandings of squats as homes.

What was certainly apparent to me even from a short period of time spent at Grow Heathrow was that, as well as a site of economic and political protest, it was very much home for the people who lived there. As discussed earlier in this chapter, the structures designed and built by the crew catered to their domestic needs. Interiors were decorated, rugs scattered the floor of the kitchen and living space, photographs and artwork hung from the walls, and handmade curtains of a variety of colours and materials adorned windows. Grow Heathrow was certainly an important site for community activism and awareness-raising around climate change. But for a relatively large group of people it was also home. Indeed, while Lily was pleased by the positive response Grow Heathrow elicited from the wider public in comparison to the usual figurations of squatters as abject deviants, she also acknowledged the danger of falling into the trap of such binary depictions. She worried that reinforcing the idea of 'good' versus 'bad' squatters was ultimately dangerous, simplifying a complex practice and ignoring the wide range of reasons why people might choose to squat.

Framings of squatters, then, even when positive, dismantle their connection with homemaking. For all participants, needing a place to call home was the primary reason for their decision to squat, no matter how politically engaged they also were. Ignoring this as a reality, even when that ignorance is well-meaning, threatens to detract from the value of squats as homes. Assumptions around the good squatter as establishing squats on the basis of environmental sustainability or political protest arguably further detach squatting from conceptions of the home. These assumptions then entrench the idea that the extreme temporariness and precarity of modern-day squats is acceptable, as they are not seen as 'true' homes.

## Normalising precarity, appropriating squatting: the rise of property guardianships

As with the other policies discussed in this book, the criminalisation of squatting is emblematic of the home as a deeply politicised, and increasingly precaritised, space. Neoliberal governance structures that infiltrate people's everyday home lives instil 'life worlds that are inflected with uncertainty and instability' (Waite 2009: 416). Section 144 is a clear example of this relationship between power hierarchies, governance practices and the everyday, enacted specifically through the site of the home. Such structures of power not only entrench precarity into the home lives of society's most vulnerable, but go so far as to normalise, even celebrate, such precarity. Gallingly, in the context of squatting this normalisation is partly achieved through a reappropriation and financialisation of the practice. This has occurred through the rising popularity of property guardianship schemes – which essentially take countercultural living and re-establish it within a neoliberal framework.

Originating in the Netherlands during the 1990s to allow cheap and temporary 'work/live' spaces for artists and students, guardianship firms are private companies that install 'property guardians' into disused (usually commercial) buildings in order to keep them 'safe' from squatters (Ferreri et al 2017). Landlords pay the firm a fee for finding the guardians, and the guardians in turn also pay the firm (usually) lower than average rent to live in the property. This lower rent is accepted on the understanding that guardians can be given just two weeks' notice (maximum)[10] to vacate, and are completely void of any tenancy rights. Therefore, just as squatting has been criminalised, so too has it simultaneously been repurposed for commercial means under the guise of guardianship schemes. Property guardianship firms promote the schemes under the premise of a cheap cost of living, the chance to inhabit unusual and interesting spaces, and as an enactment of social responsibility – that the properties will be protected from the threat of squatters (Ferreri et al 2017; Ferreri and Dawson 2018). According to Camelot, one of the best known guardianship firms: 'Property owners turn to us to manage their vacant properties, looking to deter squatters and avoid vandalism. This in turn gives Camelot access to some of the UK's most exciting and sought after buildings' (Camelot Europe 2015).

Even politically left-wing media such as *The Guardian* have tended to promote guardianship schemes relatively uncritically as something of an adventure, an opportunity to live in and revive unusual properties (Norwood 2010). Guardianships then, go beyond the normalisation of precarious urban living, to its active celebration.

Property guardianships are a potent contribution to the destruction of squatting, reducing the number of potential squats. This is a particularly prevalent issue in the post-section 144 landscape, where the majority of squatters now deem residential properties off-limits due to the threat of arrest and fining. As the majority of guardianship properties are commercial buildings, this further reduces squatters' ability to find and establish homes. One participant, Harry, admitted to me that he had in fact abandoned squatting and moved into a guardianship. Squatting had become increasingly difficult, and becoming a property guardian was the only alternative he could afford. Despite the commercial nature of guardianship schemes, Harry felt he was left with little option in the face of an ever-declining squatting movement. He saw becoming a guardian as the closest thing to squatting that he could manage, at least for the time being. Guardianship schemes therefore play an interesting role at the, somewhat paradoxical, intersection of increasing demand for affordable housing, and the stripping away of affordable options through legislation such as section 144. Guardianships serve an ominous dual function, a means of remaining in the city in the short term, while simultaneously contributing to the further reduction of viable non-financialised homespaces in the long term (Nowicki 2021).[11] Harry's decision is a controversial one among squatters, who often see moving into guardianships as something of a cultural and ideological betrayal. As Dave remarked, "I think moving into a guardianship is a sure-fire way to lose friends!" However, Dave's crewmate Matteo sympathised with people like Harry, acknowledging that squatting is becoming an increasingly unsustainable struggle, and that the move of some squatters into guardianship schemes may therefore be a somewhat inevitable consequence of section 144.

Alongside property guardianships reducing the number of suitable buildings available to squatting crews whilst normalising precarious urban housing structures more broadly, they also aesthetically appropriate squatting as a cultural practice. The appeal of life as a property guardian in part lies in the opportunity to live in unusual buildings, for example former warehouses or schools, and to live communally, often with a relatively large number of people. This ethos of communal living and the creative reuse of empty property is clearly aligned with elements of squatting culture. Guardianship schemes are therefore an appropriation of the aesthetics of squatting, while at the same time being completely at odds with its political ethics. More broadly, guardianship schemes contribute to an aesthetic urban trend, particularly in the post-recession climate, that envisions temporariness and the repurposing of property as inherently positive and entrepreneurial (Harris 2015, 2020). This is notable in the commercial, as well as housing, sectors, particularly in relation to the rise of the 'pop-up' phenomenon, a now somewhat ubiquitous term that largely denotes the interim use of vacant commercial properties. Pop-up bars, shops and cafes have become commonplace in London, particularly in gentrified, or gentrifying, parts of the city, generally attracting a young, white, middle-class clientele. Along with guardianships, their aesthetic is relatively consistent and easily recognisable, despite occupying a wide array of building types. This often includes a 'shabby chic' appearance, for example through exposed brickwork and mismatched furniture, and the retention of some objects or style that allude to the building's past use (Harris 2012). For example, an acquaintance of mine lived as a property guardian in a former pub in east London, still decked out with bar and dartboard, pub sign still hanging from the side of the building, despite the fact that it had been out of business for several years. This trend can in part be understood as a form of 'post-recession gentrification', whereby a neighbourhood's working-class heritage and history is repurposed for wealthier incomers (Lees 2000). This is what Andrew Harris terms 'the production and re-imagining of urban space for more affluent social groups' (2012: 235). These aesthetics are consciously drawn on in pop-up and guardianship marketing strategies, but are also something of an incidental by-product of squatting. Although very much politically and culturally opposed to one another, there are nonetheless connections between squatting and these gentrification processes. In a discussion we had about some of the changes taking place within the squatting scene, and London more broadly, Dave acknowledged and expressed concern about this connection. He both defended and lamented the relationship between squatting and gentrification: "There are definitely tensions between gentrification and squatting. Squatting is anti-gentrification, but feeds into it at the same time. Squatting can generate an 'edgy culture'. But we haven't got any control over that."

Dave's acknowledgement of the relationship between squatter and gentrification aesthetics points to a form of domicide that is particularly ominous, whereby the practice of squatting is slowly strangled by forms of marketing and sale strategies that feed off some of the very ideals and aesthetics embedded within it. During my time at Dave's squat, this was one of the few points during our conversation when he appeared somewhat defeated, seemingly frustrated by the cruel irony that the aesthetics of his lifestyle are in some ways inspiring gentrification practices that are contributing to the decimation of affordable housing.[12]

The growing precaritisation of squatting due to section 144, and the implementation of schemes such as property guardianships that further deconstruct squatting culture, have left a marked strain on those who continue to maintain squatting as a homemaking practice. This is everyday domicide at its most literal and material. As section 144 makes the risk of squatting empty residential properties too great, and guardianship schemes monopolise London's empty commercial properties, squatting threatens to be reduced to an extinct subculture.

This commercialisation of precarious living also further strengthens the financialisation of housing, in turn extending moralised perceptions of squatters as socially parasitical. The acceptance of insecure tenancies and precarious housing as the status quo engenders further resentment towards those leading alternative – and particularly rent- and mortgage-free – lifestyles. Such normalisation of precarious housing is a mode of governance that ultimately reframes expectations of home. Where once affordable housing for life formed one of the bastions of post-Second World War society in the UK, now those who want or need to live in cheaper housing are expected to embrace temporary and precarious lifestyles.

The most concerning domicidal aspects of section 144, then, do not solely lie in the immediate impacts of increased forced eviction discussed earlier in the chapter, although these are of course crucial elements. But the *socio-symbolic* component of domicide, too, stands to have a long-term impact on the home lives of London's low-income and vulnerable residents. Processes of domicide should not be understood solely as the physical destruction of or displacement from the homespace, but also as a rhetorically charged process whereby particular types of home are dismantled through structuring them and their occupants as morally dubious. Taking this one step further, property guardianships enact socio-symbolic domicide by producing a rhetoric that at once constructs squatting as something that property owners need to be protected from, and as a fetishised lifestyle that can be profited from. This is arguably where domicide becomes most dangerous and concretised, as the decimation of an alternative homemaking practice is legitimised, and its commercialisation simultaneously celebrated. In short, squatting has been dismantled, and its skin used to establish a new precarious, glamourised housing typology. When domicide is reconstructed as positive in such a way, the consequences are far-reaching, dismantling not only individual homes, but our expectations of what a home can and should be.

# 5

# Fighting for home: activism and resistance in precarious times

Across the last few chapters I have examined the various ways in which UK housing policy enacts domicide on working-class, low-income and vulnerable people. This chapter takes a slightly different approach, exploring the multitude of ways in which these domicidal policies have been fought and resisted. The resistive tools and techniques outlined here are varied in their strategies and scope – from legal challenges, to hiding in plain sight to avoid forced eviction, to actively using forced eviction as a means of exposing housing injustice, to the role of material objects in creating home in hostile environments. What all of these forms of resistance do have in common is the determination to fight for a right to home for all.

## Using law and policy as tools of resistance

This book has so far highlighted how legislative and policy changes are deployed to purposefully strip away the homemaking abilities of working-class and low-income people. And yet, just as law and policy can be used to further urban spatial injustice, they can also be reworked as tools of resistance. Scholars such as David Delaney, Nicholas Blomley and Katherine Brickell have called for social scientists to investigate these 'contingencies and constraints of social justice' (Delaney 2016: 267) in order to better understand the ways in which the law, in particular, can be used to resist spatial injustice. I argue that much of this work is already being done by the victims of domicidal policies, through grassroot networks that reshape legal and policy barriers into tools of resistance. The following section of this chapter focuses on the multifaceted ways in which housing injustice is challenged through legal and policy frameworks.

### Legally challenging the bedroom tax

Challenging the bedroom tax through legal means has proved to be a prevalent, and often successful, method of resistance. In doing so, social tenants affected by the bedroom tax and their advocates have de-legitimised the government's actions using the same frameworks that have been designed to penalise them. As highlighted in Chapter 2, legal challenges to the bedroom tax have taken place on a range of scales. This use of the law as a method of resistance to the bedroom tax can be found at every level of the national court system. Since its implementation, the policy has been contested in both First-tier and Upper-tier Tribunals[1] on a wide range of grounds: from discrimination against disabled people, in particular those who need overnight care, specialist equipment storage, or separate rooms from partners; to discrimination against single parents who do not have primary custody of their children; to appeals on the grounds of rooms being too small or of an inappropriate shape to be considered a bedroom.

Legal challenges to the bedroom tax have also been considered in both the Court of Appeal and the Supreme Court, the highest in the UK legal system. One of the better-known early cases was that of the Carmichaels. Jacqueline Carmichael has spina bifida – her husband, also her 24-hour carer, sleeps in a separate room because of her condition. Despite their medical need for two bedrooms, the couple received a 14 per cent reduction in their housing benefit eligibility as a consequence of the bedroom tax. They took their case to court, and at a Tribunal hearing in April 2014 a judge ruled that the Carmichaels were entitled to two bedrooms, and that the bedroom tax should not have been imposed. In the same year, a group of disabled tenants, including the Carmichaels, took their cases to the Court of Appeal on the grounds that the bedroom tax was a curtailment of their human rights. The Court ruled against their case, stating that 'although the under-occupancy rules were discriminatory, for disabled adults the discrimination was justified and therefore lawful' (Leigh Day 2014). However, in January 2016, the Court of Appeal went on to rule in favour of two other parties penalised by the bedroom tax, on the grounds that in their cases the policy was unlawful. The plaintiffs were the grandparents of a teenager who needed overnight care, and a victim of domestic violence, known as 'A', whose 'spare room' is a panic room installed by the police to protect her from a violent ex-partner (BBC 2016). A further victory was won in November 2016, when the same group whose case had been rejected by the Court of Appeal won in the Supreme Court. The Supreme Court ruling now means that social tenants with similar disabilities where partners need to sleep in separate rooms, people who act as overnight carers for disabled family members, or who have panic rooms installed, are able to challenge the legality of their penalisation through the bedroom tax using the Supreme Court ruling as case-based evidence. This was strengthened further by another Supreme Court case in 2019, where the Court ruled that a man, known as RR, should not be subject to the bedroom tax as it is a curtailment of his human rights. Alongside this, it was ruled that it is not legal for local authorities to apply the bedroom tax in cases where it would lead to a breach of the Human Rights Act (Leigh Day 2019). Legal challenges to the bedroom tax went further still in the same year, when 'A' took their case to The European Court of Human Rights, who ruled that the policy unlawfully discriminates against victims of domestic violence (Hopkin Murray Beskine 2020). The Court ruled that 'A' was particularly prejudiced by the bedroom tax because of her gender, and that the policy was in conflict with the aims of police protection schemes for victims of domestic violence. The Court also noted the UK government did not provide any 'weighty reasons' to justify the discrimination.

The success of these legal challenges highlights the ways in which law can be used to expose and redress spatial injustice. In the examples of these high-profile cases, their challenges to the bedroom tax focused on the ways in which the policy discriminates against disabled people and those protecting themselves from domestic violence, asking the courts to redraw understandings of the 'spare bedroom'. In many instances, these bedrooms were revealed to be necessary spaces for the assurance of wellbeing and safety for individuals for a multitude of reasons beyond sleep. The challenges brought to the fore the ways in which governments discriminate against groups who are often already marginalised or vulnerable. Legal challenges to the bedroom tax have, in particular, highlighted the ways in which such policies discount the spatial and architectural needs of those who are marginalised by a political discourse that understands homemaking solely through the lens of non-disabled needs and the idealised nuclear family (Imrie 2014).

### Virtual legal spaces: the role of social media in legally challenging the bedroom tax

Reworking the law from a barrier to an aid has been a useful tool of resistance against the bedroom tax not only in high-profile cases. A prominent method of legal resistance also lies in the use of social media, in particular Facebook groups, that provide support and information. People who join these groups post details of their specific circumstances and ask other members for advice regarding how they might appeal their local authority's decision to implement the bedroom tax. For example, many people often post queries relating to the size and shape of their rooms, looking for advice on whether they are able to launch an appeal on the basis that what their local authority has deemed a 'spare bedroom' is in fact too small to be classed as such. Other group members post previous disputes that tenants have won on various grounds in order to help people build their cases, as the pinned post for one group highlights:

> What size is the room? Is it under 65.81 square feet. after deducting unusable floor space – for door opening, radiators, boxing, stairwell etc.? Can you easily fit a bed and basic bedroom furniture in there? Is there a boiler in the room? Are there any safety issues with it being

used to sleep in? What about the shape? Is there a sloping ceiling? Would the bed be too near, or obstructing, the radiator?

The room should be capable of accommodating a single adult bed, a bedside table and somewhere to store clothes (see paragraph 33 of Nelson), as well as providing space for dressing and undressing. ... Use the appeal letter ... then once you've filled this in you need to print it off and sign it and hand it in to your local council (NOT your landlord, but your local council). Get a receipt for it, or, if posting, post by recorded delivery, and keep a copy.

Using amalgamated knowledge of tribunal decisions on bedroom tax appeal cases, group members encourage one another to take action and appeal local authority decisions. Here, social media demystifies the court room – a space usually understood as a site of resistance only for those who have high levels of economic and social capital. Social media in this instance reconstructs the courtroom as an attainable site through which resistance to the bedroom tax can be sought and rights to home re-established. Through grassroots-level legal organisation, social tenants are able to build the legal knowledge and skills to challenge the bedroom tax, one case at a time. This is an example of what the sociologist Alain Touraine terms active citizenship – defined as citizens demanding agency. Active citizenship captures the emergence of actors that demand to be recognised as subjects in their own right, rather than being reduced to passive 'subjects of the state' (Touraine 2000). In this instance, social media acts as a particularly useful means of establishing such agency, particularly among communities who have low incomes and are disproportionately living with disabilities. This is because social media is largely accessible, and people are less likely to be limited by social, economic and mobility constraints to protesting and resistance.

The phenomenon of social media as a key contemporary site of resistance and dissent has garnered particular academic interest over the last decade. This was sparked in particular by the 2011 Arab Spring and global Occupy movement, the first high-profile instances of social media's role in global political activism (Gerbaudo 2012). Indeed, social media is often in part attributed to the overthrowing of dictators in Egypt, Tunisia, Morocco and Libya during the Arab Spring (Tudoroiu 2014). However, since 2011, the optimistic stance that social media is a positive tool for change has been complicated. Rises in far-right political extremism, the 2016 election of Donald Trump in the USA, and rampant COVID-19 conspiracies have been heavily facilitated by Facebook and other major social media platforms. Despite this expansion of social media's political usage, it nonetheless continues to provide an integral means of resistance for people who are often socially and spatially marginalised. Social media support groups are an important means of circumventing socioeconomic geographic barriers. Social tenants who may not have otherwise been able to become involved in organised resistance are empowered through the construction of a network formed on the basis of a shared struggle and desire to challenge diminished rights to home.

Mobilities scholarship has identified sociality and community identity as being produced through networks of people and ideas that cannot necessarily be ascribed to living in close geographical proximity (Cresswell 2010). This, too, can be said of (im)mobility and exclusion from traditional spaces of resistance such as the street or public square. Communities that are unbound by spatial fixity can become key sites through which to challenge domicide and reclaim rights to home. The online bedroom tax support groups work to de-mythologise and reframe the legal spaces of the city from spaces of intimidation to spaces of emancipation. This is achieved through encouraging members to appeal the bedroom tax and thus enter the court system. As the pinned post for one support group states: 'Our aim is to help you appeal the bedroom tax and gain exemption from it. There are thousands of tenants who are now bedroom tax free, due to doing just that. ... Remember ... Appealing the bedroom tax and gaining exemption from it, is Permanent.'

First-tier or Upper-tier Tribunal appeals are dealt with on a case-by-case basis, and are much smaller in scale than the Supreme Court hearings in terms of their potential for immediate and widespread change. They are nonetheless crucial spaces through which social tenants can potentially regain autonomy over their homes, and pave the way for others to do the same. The Facebook groups do not evoke a public spectacle of resistance like the Supreme Court cases. They do, however, seek to entrench and normalise the confidence to challenge the bedroom tax. This emphasis on both a long-term solution to the bedroom tax for individuals, and encouraging the utilisation of collective legal knowledge, encapsulates a form of resistance where piecemeal actions can lead to bigger outcomes (Katz 2004). In this way, the continual challenging and dismantling of the law that underpins the bedroom tax has the potential to eventually erode the legal legitimacy of the policy altogether.

### Finding other means: Discretionary Housing Payments and legal loopholes

It is not just tenants themselves who have used legislation as a means of resisting the bedroom tax. Housing associations and housing and welfare charities have also provided support for people through the use of legal loopholes and the reappropriation of other forms of state financial provision. DHP, a pot of funding allocated to local authorities to provide housing support, as well as other forms of welfare support such as Tax Credits and ESA, have been used where possible to cover the shortfalls created by the bedroom tax.

Throughout my research, I found that support organisations themselves also often faced precarious outcomes as a consequence of the bedroom tax, particularly housing associations through a loss of income from tenants. There were, therefore, high levels of motivation to find ways of working around the policy. Employees of housing associations and charities that I interviewed often talked of the varying ways in which they tried to offset the worst effects of the bedroom tax. In 2014 I spoke with the welfare officer for a small housing association managing properties predominantly in an east London borough with high levels of deprivation. She told me that her organisation had thus far managed to avoid evicting anyone as a consequence of the bedroom tax, and that this was largely due to the existence of DHP. Indeed, all housing associations I spoke with cited DHP as the most common and effective means of reducing the impact of the bedroom tax in the short-to-medium term. For many housing associations, re-routing DHP funding, previously used mainly for private tenants rather than those in the social rented sector, was an essential means of ensuring as little impact as possible for those affected by the bedroom tax.

A welfare and debt adviser for a UK debt charity confirmed that DHP provided a vital source of relief for clients affected by the bedroom tax. He helped people apply to their local authority for DHP funding, as well as looking into whether they were eligible for further Tax Credits or higher levels of ESA in order to make up some of the income lost. In this way, housing associations and charities have developed strategies that mitigate the worst effects of the bedroom tax by using state financial support – combatting the loss of income in one area of the welfare system by attempting to extract more resources from another. Similarly to the example of the Facebook support groups, this is an approach that utilises legal and policy knowledge to subvert and challenge the bedroom tax.

This was also evident in the emergence of a legal loophole in the bedroom tax legislation which housing associations and charities capitalised on in order to help clients claim back income lost. '[P]aragraph 4(1)(a) of Schedule 3 of the Housing Benefit and Council Tax Benefit (Consequential Provisions) Regulations 2006' effectively exempted tenants who have been continuously in receipt of housing benefit at the same address since 1 January 1996 (Wilson 2016).[2] This again enabled those working in housing support to employ legal frameworks to reduce the impact of the bedroom tax. Indeed, one housing association welfare officer informed me that at least 30 households he worked with had been exempted from the bedroom tax as a consequence of the loophole.

However, while such commitment to mitigating the harms caused by the bedroom tax and enabling people to remain in their homes is commendable, these methods are ultimately short-term and responsive, rather than transformative, in their approach. Reliance on DHP as a mitigation strategy is particularly precarious, as DHP funding allocations from central government continue to be cut. Although DHP funding was increased from £139.5 million to £180 million in 2020/21 as a consequence of the coronavirus pandemic, it has since been cut back to £140 million for the 2021/22 financial year – a reduction of 22 per cent, and lower than previous budgets in 2017/18 and 2018/19 (Jayanetti 2021). The reality is that the utilisation of other forms of housing support as a method of resistance can only go so far when these too are being dismantled by the government.

### Unionising the unregulated: legal challenges in the private rented sector

Undoubtedly, the bedroom tax regularly penalises socially and financially marginalised people. Despite this, the sheer unfairness of the policy has meant that legal challenges on the grounds of discrimination and what actually constitutes a bedroom have regularly been successful. But how do activists legally challenge discrimination and malpractice within a housing tenure as unregulated as the private rented sector? The short answer is, with difficulty. Legislation such as section 21 of the 1980 Housing Act discussed in Chapter 3 means that it is perfectly legal to evict people at short notice and without reason. If this is acceptable legal practice within the private rented sector, then legislative avenues of resistance are inevitably limited.

Nonetheless, over the past decade a range of grassroots unions and direct action groups have formed around the issue, particularly in London. This includes Digs, the renters' union for the borough of Hackney. Digs was set up when one of its founding members decided to call a meeting for private renters in the borough after a string of bad experiences with landlords (Wilde 2019). Initial group activities included undertaking training in housing law, and using their new knowledge to run renters' 'skill-ups' to help people identify and resist illegal eviction and mistreatment by landlords. Shortly after the founding of Digs, the Radical Housing Network emerged, helping to forge a network of housing activist groups across the country, and further galvanising local organisations to provide a range of support for private renters. This has included letters to MPs, protests and blockading bailiffs.

As making legal challenges against landlords is particularly difficult in such a highly unregulated market, renters' organisations often focus on performative tactics to publicly highlight housing injustice. For example, in 2016 Digs launched the #YesDSS[3] campaign to challenge the extremely common practice of private landlords refusing to rent their properties to people in receipt of housing benefit. This was at the time perfectly legal, despite the fact that it is blatantly discriminatory. The campaign's actions included: people giving public speeches about their experiences of being denied accesses to private rented accommodation because of their benefits status; a 'mystery shopper' experiment that found just one out of 50 letting agents approached rented out properties to people in receipt of housing benefit; and flash occupations of Hackney letting agents, demanding explanations for this discrimination (Wilde 2019). As Matt Wilde notes in his ethnographic study of Digs, the campaign 'highlighted the numerous legal and institutional barriers that stood in the way of significant PRS reform' (2019: 75).

While confronting discrimination in the private rented sector through legal frameworks remains difficult, there have nonetheless been some significant inroads in recent years. In July 2020, District Judge Victoria Mark ruled that blanket bans on renting properties to people on housing benefit is unlawful (Richardson 2020). The ruling found that a single mother of two, whose case was taken on by Shelter, had experienced indirect discrimination when a letting agent refused to rent to her. This sets an important precedent for the many people experiencing similar discrimination. A year later, in July 2021, a further legal milestone was reached by a group of private tenants living in a block in Hackney owned by the billionaire property magnate John Christodoulou. A housing tribunal ordered that Christodoulou pay £19,000 to the group for failing to correctly license his property as an HMO (household of multiple occupancy) (Brown 2021). The group utilised the rent repayment order (RRO), a little-known legal mechanism that, since 2004, has meant renters are entitled to reimbursement of up to one year's rent if their landlord has failed to license an HMO. As the block is almost entirely owned by the same landlord, this opens up the possibility of many more of Christodoulou's tenants taking him to court under RROs. As we saw with paragraph 4(1)(a) of Schedule 3 of the Housing Benefit and Council Tax Benefit (Consequential Provisions) Regulations 2006 in relation to the bedroom tax, legal loopholes can provide an important means of challenging housing injustice. Organised legal resistance continues to build as increasing numbers of people from a range of backgrounds are exposed to the atrocities of the private rented sector. In London, the 2018 formation of the London Renters' Union, a conglomerate of the Radical Housing Network, Digs and other activist groups, has helped to bring to the fore the need for sweeping legal and institutional change to the private rented sector. The spotlighting of private rental sector precarity by these groups has contributed to developments such as the 2022 publication of the 'Fairer Private Rented Sector' White Paper mentioned in Chapter 1 – although at the time of writing it remains unclear whether any of its recommendations will be taken further by the government. Ultimately, establishing wide-scale change through the law remains challenging when so little legal protection exists for private renters in the first place.

### Legally challenging section 144

Squatters have also long utilised the law as a means of challenging anti-squatting legislation, and as a space through which to fight for their autonomy and rights to home (Finchett-Maddock 2014). As already discussed in

Chapter 4, squatting's legal position has always been precarious, even before its partial illegalisation. This somewhat permanent state of precarity in large part encouraged the formation during the 1960s and 70s of longstanding resistance and advisory groups such as the ASS and the London Squatters Campaign, who have often focused their support around providing squatters with legal knowledge. For example, the 1977 Criminal Law Act left many people at the time unsure as to whether squatting had been made illegal. ASS responded to the law by launching the Squatting Is Still Legal campaign in 1978 to reassure squatters that the practice remained a civil, rather than criminal, offence.

As explored in the previous chapter, in his vitriolic anti-squatting speech in 2011, then-MP Mike Weatherley denounced squatters for 'running rings around the law'. And indeed, it can be argued that there is some kernel of truth to this. Due to their hyper-precarious state, squatters often have high levels of legal knowledge, which they utilise to protect their homes, and the homes of fellow squatters. In his account of London's squatting movement in the 1960s and 70s, Ron Bailey recalled an incident where a group of squatters used their legal expertise to trick the police, and thus save themselves from eviction. They complied with a possession order on a squatted building by moving one family out and another in. This meant that when the police came to evict the squatters, they found they could no longer do so as the possession order was against a family that was no longer there (Bailey 1973). The 1977 law change was also used to encourage amnesty between the Greater London Council (GLC)[4] and squatter groups, with the GLC making the decision to legalise and license 1,850 squats rather than deal with the mass eviction, and subsequent rehousing, of thousands of people (Finchett-Maddock 2014). Such tactics highlight the longstanding relationship between squatting and the law, with the law acting as both a barrier to squatting, and a means through which to resist eviction and displacement.

More recently, SQUASH was formed in 2011 to challenge the impending law change. The group consisted of legal scholars, social scientists and activists. When I met Roberta, a key member of the group, in summer 2014, she told me about their attempts to challenge the legal, social and economic viability of section 144. On the basis that no impact assessment had been conducted by the government, in 2013 SQUASH developed their own impact assessment six months after section 144's implementation. The report, *The Case Against Section 144*, was endorsed by academics (Danny Dorling, Alex Vasudevan and Kesia Reeve), MP (and former shadow chancellor of the exchequer) John McDonnell and Liberal Democrat Baroness Miller.

Its findings condemned the legislation on four key policy and legal grounds. First, the report argued that the law's implementation had been undemocratic, and thus legally dubious, due to the overly short parliamentary process leaving little time for scrutiny. Second, it suggested that the law change was unjust as it would disproportionately impact homeless people, and place undue additional pressure on local authorities already struggling to supply housing to those in need. Third, SQUASH highlighted the adequacy of prior legislation, in particular the Criminal Law Act 1977, in protecting tenants and homeowners and restricting squatting. This raised questions as to the necessity of the law change, suggesting that section 144 was ideological, rather than the pragmatic protective act it claimed to be. Finally, the report suggested that section 144 is unaffordable, citing direct (evictions, arrests and prosecutions) and indirect (increased welfare expenditure, particularly in relation to housing benefit) costs that the law change incites. This highlighted that the law was at direct odds with austerity policymaking agendas (SQUASH 2013). SQUASH continued to provide reports listing the yearly arrests made under section 144, and highlighting the relationship between the law change and rising rates of homelessness until 2016. Similar groups such as the Squatters Legal Network have also tailed off in their online publication and posting presence in recent years, indicating that capacity and demand for legal advice has slowly reduced as section 144 has taken hold. While this is a rather bleak prognosis for the squatting scene, the practice's relationship with the law remains an important one, both as a barrier to and facilitator of, alternative homemaking.

## Invisible resistance

Throughout this book, I have examined how domicidal policies have impacted squatters and tenants of social and private rented housing, and considered the connections between these seemingly disparate groups. However, there remains a clear difference in the levels of demonisation and othering of squatters due to their assumed status as criminals. This has, in part, meant that squatters have been forced to use a wider, and at times more covert, array of resistive tools, often with a focus on reworking the practice in order to ensure its survival. Squatters have struggled to garner public sympathy in the wake of section 144, and there is little political appetite, even from the left, to challenge the law. In the months immediately before and after the implementation of section 144, SQUASH had made repeated attempts to gain the support of major national housing charities, but with little effect. Unlike the bedroom tax and precarity in the private rented sector, which regularly garners public concern from both the political left and housing and homelessness charities, section 144 has remained on the sidelines. In part as a consequence of this, squatters have been forced to adopt nuanced and creative methods in order to keep the practice alive. One way of doing this has been through hiding in plain sight. Remaining undetected can prove difficult for squatters in the post-criminalisation landscape, as the vast majority now live in commercial, rather than residential, properties. This immediately makes their presence more visible – in large part because squatted commercial properties tend to consist of larger crews. As commercial buildings are not ordinarily associated with having residents, any activity that indicates people are living in one makes squatting crews more visible and, as a consequence, more vulnerable to eviction.

A crew I met who were squatting a former pub in south London had dealt with their increased visibility in a particularly ingenious way. Rather than trying to make the property look empty, they instead embraced and appropriated its visibility by masking the building's usage as something other than a home, therefore protecting themselves from eviction. As Tariq showed me when I met him outside the squat, the crew had made and mounted a sign over the doorway with a picture of a bike and the wording 'Bike Curious'. Tariq told me, somewhat gleefully: "We're pretending that we're running a business … and the nature of the fake business fits into gentrifier and hipster aesthetics." Indeed, this was a successful strategy as far as I was concerned – I had been confused by the sign until Tariq had come out to meet me, as I thought I was in the wrong place for the interview. Interestingly, the crew were employing gentrification tropes and reappropriating them to protect their home, and they believed that in part as a consequence of this the squat had received very little unwanted interest from locals or police. By making their homespace invisible through connecting the squat with hipster and gentrification aesthetics – the road-bike being emblematic of hipsterism – Tariq and his crew had used the very same sociopolitical structures that have led to the displacement of many of inner London's low-income residents in order to secure a home for themselves. In doing this, the crew had subverted such aesthetics in order to disguise themselves as a hipster trope, and thus avoid public detection.

Rather than fearing the increased precarity that arose from their unavoidable visibility, Tariq and his crew chose instead to subvert their precarious condition by hiding in plain sight – a strategy that became the means of their squat's continued existence. This battle to survive in the post-criminalisation landscape is, I argue, a form of resistance in and of itself. The crew's method mimicked now common imaginings of inner London, whereby gentrification has brought about the displacement of many residents. The related hipster aesthetics of gentrification, often ironically drawn from squatter culture and style, have commercialised and contributed to the erasure of many of the cultural practices they have been inspired by. But by engaging with and appropriating some of the very sociopolitical conditions that have contributed to the increased precaritisation of squatters and other low-income groups, the crew were ultimately able to protect themselves from the threat of forced eviction. As the geographer Alex Vasudevan notes, squatting 'points to the possibilities – complex, makeshift and experimental – for extending, improving and sustaining life in settings of pervasive marginality' (2015: 354). Within its very confines as a precarious and marginal practice, squatting ekes out alternative forms of belonging and rights to the city (Vasudevan 2015). This proves to be particularly invaluable in a political landscape that has confined those deemed appropriate urban dwellers to those who subscribe to neoliberal ideals – sidelining, rejecting and criminalising those who seek out different understandings of, and modes of belonging in, the city. In this way, squatters are able to deploy precarity itself as a means of resistance in the everyday. Through engaging with and reworking the very constructions of inner-city gentrification and 'hipsterisation' that threaten squatting and other low-income homemaking practices, the crew constructed themselves as ubiquitous, and thus safe, in the urban landscape. This incident also highlights the ways in which home *un*making, too, can form the basis for resistance in the fact of domicidal policies (Baxter and Brickell 2014). In this case, the crew used homemaking and home unmaking simultaneously to construct a meaningful and long-lasting (in squatting terms anyway) home. By removing all external semblances of the squat as a place of residence, they were better able to establish and protect their home.

## "I see myself as more of an occupier": reappropriation as resistance

Much of this book has considered the role of language and rhetoric in demonising working-class and low-income people through their housing tenure. But what also became clear throughout my research was how choices around language are used to defend, as well as destroy, people's rights to home.

When I asked Harry a question about his experiences of being a squatter, he responded, unexpectedly, that he in fact did not like to define himself as such. Rather, he defined himself as an 'occupier'. He felt this difference in language use was crucial as "it can really change the conception of what someone is doing and why". Harry saw squatting and political protest as intrinsically linked to one another, and felt this should be emphasised when referring to the practice. Indeed, the majority of my squatter participants were very much politically active, involved in a range of groups, from the Occupy movement, to anti-Heathrow Airport expansion, to the Radical Housing Network. As discussed in the previous chapter, this can be a potentially unhelpful framing of squatting, once again detaching the practice from homemaking and threatening to construct squatters around 'good' vs 'bad' binaries. However, as this section will highlight, there are also benefits to this kind of rhetoric. Reframing squatting as occupation both helps keep squatting alive under section 144, and re-establishes the practice as an important tool in contemporary housing activism (Nowicki 2021).

The strong links between squatting and political activism are not surprising considering that squatting movements in England and Wales have historically been intertwined with housing crises and political upheaval – particularly in the aftermath of the Second World War. The relationship between squatting and activism remains a strong one in contemporary times, and demand for housing rights continues to be fundamental to the squatting movement (Finchett-Maddock 2014; Reeve 2015). However, in the aftermath of the implementation of section 144, attitudes towards and associations with the term 'squatting' have become particularly vitriolic, with longstanding implications of squatters as criminal figures concretised by the law change. Therefore, in a criminalised climate, squatting as a political movement has in some circumstances been reappropriated, re-emerging in a similar, yet partially hidden, guise as 'occupation'. In short, there has in recent years been an at times high-profile, and yet somewhat underhand, resurgence of squatting under the auspices of occupation. This tactic, although borrowing heavily from squatting, is not used solely for anti-section 144 activism, but rather in wider challenges to housing precarity.

This trend arguably began with the 2013 occupation of what was then the UK's most expensive council house. This was led by the direct action group Housing Action Southwark and Lambeth (HASL), who occupied the south London house on the eve of its sale by Southwark Council for nearly £3 million. In their engagement with the media, HASL specifically referred to their actions as an occupation in protest of Southwark Council's decision to sell much-needed social housing in the midst of a housing crisis in the capital. Although references to the group as squatters were not entirely absent from media coverage, descriptions of the event as an occupation, with HASL members framed as protesters, were common in news reporting (see Blunden et al 2013; Withnall 2013). HASL members also made it clear in media interviews that they did not intend to live in the property, that they all had homes to return to, and that the purpose of their occupation was purely political.

This detachment of political occupation from language pertaining to squatting works in two ways. First, it quietly deploys the practice of squatting itself as a method of resistance while reducing the chance of arrest. Second, the tactic works to protect squatting post-section 144 by distancing it from associations with home (un)making. By instead framing it as occupation, squatting is reconceived as a solely political act detached from popular public assumptions that assume squatters to be guileful home-thieves. By connecting squatting in a residential building with protests centred on the wider housing crisis, while at the same time detaching it from understandings of home, squatters are potentially able to circumvent arrest under section 144 (which notably states that it is illegal to squat in a residential building *if you intend to live there*)–both keeping the practice alive and using it to convey wider messages regarding the housing crisis. Indeed, at a meeting I attended in a squatted social centre in 2014, members of HASL were present and, referring to their occupation of the Southwark council house the previous year, explicitly suggested that protest can indeed be a tactic in the protection of residential squatting. They told the audience that when they had squatted the £3 million council house, they had largely been left alone by the police even though they were in a residential building because they had framed their actions as 'protesting' and 'occupying' rather than 'residing'.

Rob, a former London squatter, also alluded to the squatting-as-occupation tactic when he told me that he and a crew had opened up a residential building in central London in the middle of the day in full public view. This was done to provide the venue for a housing activism conference protesting against MIPIM (a four-day annual real estate exhibition usually held in Cannes, but hosted in London in 2014 and 2015). Indeed, I attended and spoke at the conference held in this squat. The conference was widely attended, the audience predominantly consisting of a mix of activists, academics and sympathetic politicians, including then-leader of the Green Party Natalie Bennett. Despite the very public nature of the residential building's use, the conference ran relatively undisturbed by police for two days. Again, here section 144 appeared to be circumvented on the basis that the building had been utilised for the purposes of political protest, rather than for residence. The fact that some people had spent at least one night sleeping there appeared to have gone unnoticed by police, perhaps due to the fact that the building had been opened up so brazenly and was very clearly hosting a public event. This tactic was used again in 2016, when members of the feminist activist group Sisters Uncut occupied an empty council flat in Hackney due to be demolished, turning it into a temporary social centre whose activities included running a breakfast club for children and parents (Hartley and Atherton 2016). One of the notices put up by the group read 'This is not a squat!! This is an occupation' – again addressing the caveat in section 144 that people are eligible for arrest only if they are occupying a property they 'intend to live in'. The squatting-as-occupation (as opposed to squatting-as-home) method has, therefore, been useful in both incorporating squatting into housing activism, and protecting squatters from arrest in the wake of section 144.

## Forced eviction as a method of resistance: the case of Focus E15

Occupation has been used as a direct action technique to highlight a wide range of housing injustices, including the mistreatment of people living in temporary accommodation. Perhaps the most well-known instance of this was the occupation of the Carpenters Estate in east London by the campaign group Focus E15. The group used the occupation method as a means of both highlighting and performing the trauma of homelessness and forced eviction, with particular emphasis on gendered housing injustice.

Focus E15 originally consisted of a group of single homeless mothers living in a hostel in the borough of Newham. When in 2013 the hostel began evicting tenants due to public funding cuts, residents were told that they would be moved as far from London as Birmingham and Hull, miles from their jobs, their children's schools and their community networks. In response, and after a chance meeting with a local subset of the Revolutionary Communist Group, the soon to be evicted women set up a campaign, protesting regularly outside Newham Council's offices. The group gained high levels of local and national media coverage which eventually led to their being rehoused in Newham rather than elsewhere (Watt 2016). In the wake of this victory, Focus E15 became involved in housing activism more broadly, and has become ubiquitous in the struggle against gentrification and displacement in Newham, and London more widely. The group's activities include running a weekly street stall and the establishment of Sylvia's Corner, a social hub and space in Stratford for the development of housing campaigns.

In September 2014, they engaged in their most well-known and widely publicised direct action campaign, occupying a disused block of flats on the Carpenters Estate in Stratford. The estate had been earmarked for demolition in order to make way for a new UCL campus. However, despite these plans falling through (in part because of the controversy of the evictions due to take place), Newham Council continued to decant residents from perfectly functional social housing under the auspices that regeneration of the site would eventually occur (Watt 2013). During the two-week occupation, the flats were broken into by Focus E15 members and opened up to the public in the form of a social centre, hosting a daily programme of events including workshops, classes and performances. Unlike the HASL occupation of the Southwark council house, the actions of Focus E15 were not referred to in media coverage as squatting (see for example, Amara 2014; Dubuis 2014). Despite the fact that an entire block of flats was occupied for two weeks, with high-profile local and national press coverage, the Focus E15 campaigners were not arrested under section 144. When Newham Council took the group to court in an attempt to evict them, they won the right to remain in the flats for the duration of their planned two-week protest. The occupation ultimately led to the successful reopening of some of the flats to people in priority housing need (Watt 2016).

The appropriation of squatting by campaign groups within the wider housing activism movement, then, appears to be a useful tool in securing both publicity and tangible gains. By confronting their experiences of domicide – their forced eviction from the hostel and threat of displacement from Newham – and making their precarious living conditions public, Focus E15 succeeded in their fight to establish new homes for others.

Although their membership has extended beyond single mothers, and their current campaigns are far-reaching across different elements of the housing crisis, the Focus E15 collective remains most well known as a gendered group. Their position in the public imaginary as young mothers being evicted and threatened with displacement far from their neighbourhoods has proved a factor in their popularity and influence. Through emphasising their position as young mothers without suitable housing to raise their children, their last semblances of home taken from them as they were set to lose proximity to family support networks, Focus E15 became emblematic of housing precarity in London. More than this, they utilised both the gender norms associated with their roles as mothers, and the domicide enacted upon them by their local authority, to shame those in power into retracting some of their decisions. As Katherine Brickell (2014) has highlighted in her work with women activists in Cambodia, both normative gender tropes and the very thing (the home) that is under threat, can be utilised as powerful tools in resistance movements. Brickell's research revealed the ways in which women protesting the demolition of their homes in the Boeung Kak Lake region of Phnom Penh deployed strategies such as wearing models of houses, nests, and other imagery associated with the domestic during their campaign. Such strategies mobilise gender norms to act as a means of shaming those enacting domicide by making public the ways in which such forced eviction strips away women's access to domestic life. Similarly, Focus E15's public positioning as mothers whose homes have been destroyed by the actions of politicians proved an invaluable tactic in their success. The use of protest aesthetics that pertain to motherhood and domestic life acts to shine a light on government actors whose political decision-making has severely dismantled the homemaking capacities of vulnerable figures in society – in this case, young single mothers.

Although the campaign work of Focus E15, Sisters Uncut, HASL and others centres on demands for fairer housing and the rights of low-income Londoners to remain in their homes, much of the squatting-as-occupation method's success conversely relies on separating the act of occupation itself from homemaking. By detaching squatting from connotations of home through positioning their actions as occupation rather than for their own immediate residential needs, these groups' actions are emblematic of the transformative potential of home, even as it is unmade – that through the loss or omission of one form of home, another can rise from its ashes (Baxter and Brickell 2014). Focus E15 and others have made public the potential of squatting to reclaim and remake space, and simultaneously rendered the practice invisible by removing any semblance of homemaking, thus avoiding any negative connotations associated with squatting. In this way, they are able to both implicitly resist section 144 and publicly challenge broader concerns of housing precarity. This places such occupations at an intriguing nexus of resistance that is both visible and invisible, homely and unhomely.

## Making home in temporary accommodation: 'banal' resistance through material objects

This chapter has so far explored the ways in which the injustices of housing precarity have been challenged through the law, and through the reconstituting of squatting. Some of the methods discussed, for example the use of social media in challenging the bedroom tax, highlighted how resistance can be enacted through the everyday. This final section returns to these more 'banal' methods, in particular those we encountered in our work with the temporary residents of PLACE/Ladywell. Their resistance strategies also made use of the everyday, but with a focus on material objects, rather than the virtual.

Temporary accommodation tends to be understood as a liminal waiting space rather than a home in its own right. This is reflected in rules around decorating temporary accommodation, and indeed private rental accommodation more broadly. These usually include bans on putting nails in, or Blu-tack on, walls, thus hugely restricting residents' ability to make even basic changes to their accommodation in order to feel more at home. This is a purposeful undermining of efforts to produce a domestic environment in challenging circumstances (Harris et al 2020). One participant, Gemma, interpreted rules against wall fixtures and hangings as an attack on the ability of residents to make home in PLACE/Ladywell. She saw the spacious store room built into each flat as further confirmation that they should hide their stuff away and not see their accommodation as home (Harris et al 2020):

'So we was told, nothing on the walls, like nothing. ... I said to the property manager, so basically you want us to leave everything in the boxes, is that what that room's for, that little cupboard, you want everything stacked up in there? And basically they just said "Yeah".'

This is a flagrant restriction on the ability of PLACE/Ladywell residents to feel at home in their new surroundings, and ignores the trauma of homelessness that they continue to endure. However, as with other cases discussed in this chapter, we found instances where this means of attacking people's homemaking capacities was repurposed as a tool of resistance. In the case of decorating temporary accommodation, tactically placed material objects were used to defiantly assert a sense of home in accommodation that restricted domestic attachment. For example, the prohibition of nails had led many residents in PLACE/Ladywell to turn to stick-on solutions.

In compensatory attempts to make the walls of the flats homely, multiple families had decided to decorate using wall stickers given they could not hang frames on the walls. As Scott explained:

'The thing is we've been told we're not allowed to put any pictures up on the walls, we're not allowed to make any holes, but we went out and got those sticky picture things ... we've ... stuck up a couple of pictures and what not. So instead of having the walls as a completely blank canvas, you know like you want it to feel like home.'

The importance placed on decorative items emphasises their significant role in strengthening emotional attachments between people and their accommodation, regardless of landlord attempts to shut this relationship down.

Gemma had a particularly memorable and powerful way of asserting her right to home in this way. She had decorated her temporary accommodation with a fireplace façade, attached to the walls with small screws that she intended to fill in when she moved out. Before visiting Gemma at PLACE/ Ladywell we had already heard about her fireplace in the media. It had gained attention from journalists and architects who had visited her flat, partly through an appreciation of its aesthetics and partly, perhaps, in comedic appreciation of Gemma's bold decorative move in a property that, designed as emergency accommodation for homeless families, people were not expected or encouraged to decorate. Gemma was pleased that people had been commenting on her fireplace: "Everybody said it just makes the room ... the fire place does make the room, doesn't it, and I'm very proud." She had originally bought the fireplace to decorate the house she had rented for many years before being made homeless. Having the fireplace in PLACE/Ladywell was very important for Gemma in terms of continuity with her old home and she had felt sad about the idea of leaving it in the storage cupboard to wait for a future property. She referred to the PLACE/ Ladywell flat as a "blank space" that was not conducive to feeling homely. As the sociologists Sarah DeWard and Angie Moe (2010) have argued, being able 'to construct and maintain a sense of self-worth' within the context of temporary accommodation 'may be critical for survival', but comes under threat when people – and women in particular – are required to live by rules that undermine their autonomy. They outline the struggles of women to assert their agency within such regulated environments, detailing how any resistance to regulations is often read as an act of insanity, on the assumption that only somebody mentally unsound would refuse to comply with what are seen as reasonable and basic rules. However, small acts of defiance such as Gemma's insistence on putting her fireplace up in PLACE/Ladywell, are, as DeWard and Moe suggest, important avowals of self-worth that should not be discounted as banal, insignificant or odd.

Much of this book has explored how purposeful limitations on homemaking are linked to the stigma faced by working-class and low-income people, who are seen as less deserving of home. Here, Gemma refuses to be stigmatised. Rather than anxiously complying with stringent rules on how the flats should be kept, she is defiantly proud of the alterations she has made. The fireplace is a way for Gemma to assert that she will not be made transient and that she will establish a sense of home regardless of what space and time she has (Harris et al 2020). This was also reflected in related research I and colleagues conducted with homeless families in Dublin where, even when families were faced with living in hotel rooms for extended periods of time, a determination to construct a sense of home remained. For our participants, this included buying personalised bedsheets so accommodation looked more like the bedroom of a house than a hotel room, and rearranging rooms to look less 'hotel-like'. For example, one participant recounted turning one of the room's twin beds into a sofa so that the room took on the aesthetic of a studio flat (Nowicki et al 2019). Such emphasis on asserting identity through objects associated with the domestic highlights the importance of homemaking, even in accommodation designed to be unhomely. Such defiant determination to make home in hostile environments reveals the strength of desire that people in precarious housing have to retain a sense of self and security. It also emphasises that the struggle for the right to home happens in myriad ways and places, in some cases visible, in others tucked away into the everyday.

To conclude, this chapter has highlighted the range of ways that people respond to and resist domicidal policies, and attempt to regain rights to home lost through government actions. The methods discussed are wide-ranging and seemingly disparate, from using social media as a pseudo-legal advice clinic, to occupying council estates. And yet what binds them together are the ways in which they place home at their centre. Home is both the place being fought for, and the tool used to fight against domicide and housing injustice.

# Conclusion

On 11 July 2016, a few weeks after the UK voted to leave the European Union – the culmination of a bitterly divisive referendum campaign – David Cameron resigned as prime minister. After giving a short speech in which he asserted his belief that the country had emerged stronger under his leadership, Cameron strolled back into No. 10 Downing Street humming a carefree tune to himself. After leaving office, the overseer of austerity Britain retreated to his £25,000 designer garden shed to write a 'tell all' memoir, while the legacy he created continues to wreak havoc on working-class and low-income lives. In six years as prime minister, David Cameron oversaw a suite of policies that decimated the lives of many. Child poverty in particular rose from 27 per cent to 30 per cent between 2011/12 and 2016/17 (Bourquin et al 2020), the public cost of which has risen by over 20 per cent since 2013 (Hirsch 2021). And yet, in the years since Cameron's departure the ongoing consequences of his austerity agenda have been sidelined as other, more eye-catching political and social changes such as Brexit and the COVID-19 pandemic took precedence. In the midst of these events consuming media attention, the continued lived experience of austerity is slowly being forgotten. Indeed, in 2018 then-Prime Minister Theresa May went so far as to declare that "austerity is over" (PoliticsHome 2018). More recently, this was echoed by former Chancellor of the Exchequer, now Prime Minister, Rishi Sunak, who in his October 2021 autumn budget speech declared that Boris Johnson's government had established "an economy fit for a new age of optimism" (Sunak 2021).

And yet, the consequences of austerity politics continue to ricochet through the lives of ordinary people. At the 2021 Royal Geographical Society Annual Conference, I attended sessions organised by geographers Sander van Lanen and Sarah Marie Hall that reflected on the myriad legacies of austerity. Topics ranged from Tom Disney and Ian Robson's research on the erosion of state family support; to Stephanie Denning's work examining the vital role of foodbanks in feeding low-income people; to Meredith Whitten's exploration of how austerity cuts have led to the commercialisation and declining quality of public green spaces. These sessions writ large the reality that, although we have begun to talk about austerity in the past tense as other, shinier problems take precedence, Cameron's war on welfare is very much an ongoing reality for many people. This has been compounded yet further by the emergence in 2022 of a cost of living crisis that has seen energy prices skyrocket to unprecedented levels, inflation reach a 40-year high, and wages continue to stagnate. In the current economic climate, those who were already living extremely precarious lives as a consequence of austerity and welfare 'reform' policies are being plunged further into poverty.

One of the key ways in which austerity continues to linger is in relation to housing and home. The bedroom tax continues largely unchallenged, family homelessness and reliance on temporary accommodation provision continues to soar, and alternative means of accessing housing, such as squatting, remain out of bounds for most. More broadly, average house prices continue to diverge at stunning pace from average wages, the overpriced and insecure private rented sector continues wildly unchecked, and the construction of genuinely affordable housing remains near non-existent. And the notion that some (that is, middle-class, 'professional') people deserve home more than others (namely, working-class, low-income people) continues to be normalised, with homeownership remaining a supposed policy priority despite its increasingly widespread unattainability.

## Academic and policy contributions

However, as this book attests, particularly in Chapter 1, the destruction of home for working-class and low-income people certainly did not begin in 2008. Decades of neoliberal ideology that constructs home as a site of individual ownership and financial investment has simultaneously dismissed huge swathes of the population as unproductive, un-valuable, and therefore undeserving of a decent home. Social tenants, low-income families and squatters are maligned and discredited on the basis of their housing choices (or lack thereof), left to face the threat of forced eviction, spiral into mental health crises, and forced to 'prove' themselves as worthy of existing in London and other high-cost parts of the country. The stories and experiences outlined in this book highlight how a wide range of Londoners are being denied the right to home. I argue that it is this dismantling of low- (and increasingly middle-)income people's ability to secure and maintain affordable, long-term homes in the capital that lies at the heart of London's supposed housing crisis. What we are witnessing is not merely a crisis born out of post-crash national debt, nor austerity as the logical response to a bloated welfare state. These are the consequences of active decision-making and narrativising by successive governments that, over many decades, has established some lives as more worthy of home than others.

This book has highlighted how the bedroom tax, rises in family homelessness and reliance on temporary accommodation provision, and the criminalisation of squatting contribute to three key areas of policy interest. First is the changing nature of welfare in the UK, and the role of policy rhetoric in shaping public attitudes towards working-class and low-income people. Second, it strengthens understanding of the impacts of these three policy changes on people's everyday lives – a regularly overlooked element of policy evaluation. Third, it highlights the multifaceted ways in which these policies have been challenged and resisted by both those directly affected, and their advocates.

Conceptually, this research has contributed to and furthered the critical geographies of home sub-field in two key ways. First, I have sought in my discussions of the home to extend understandings of domicide – the intentional destruction of home – beyond solely the destruction of, or displacement from, the physical dwelling. Rather, I have considered the ways in which homemaking capacities are destroyed through language and narrative. In the context of the book's three case studies, I highlighted the ways in which domicide is enacted through political rhetoric that frames social tenants, homeless families and squatters as undeserving of home. Such rhetoric, in turn, justifies these policies as morally sound. This is a process I have termed socio-symbolic domicide. I argue that this is a crucial addition to understandings of domicide as it encapsulates the ways in which the concept of home is used to disrupt and diminish people's rights to decent and secure housing.

A second key contribution of the book to social sciences scholarship is how it strengthens connections between critical geographies of home and housing studies. An ongoing lack of dialogue between the two disciplines, despite their clear relationship, has produced a disconnection between research on home and socioeconomic studies of housing, with the home often seen as an intangible and apolitical concept, and therefore at times dismissed. In this book, I have sought to place the home at the centre of understanding housing policy. In particular, I have highlighted the power of language and rhetoric that lauds middle-class homeowners and derides those who cannot, or will not, ascribe to these ideals. I argue that discussion of housing policy through the lens of the home encourages wider understanding beyond its economic implications. A focus on how the ideal home is narrativised in housing policy reveals long-term societal effects beyond housing markets alone. Taking seriously the home as an important political tool elucidates how different groups of people are categorised and (de)valued by the governments who are supposed to advocate for them. Housing and home are clearly intrinsically connected. To dismiss or underplay the role of the home in shaping housing policy decisions, and in turn the impact that housing policy has on how we construct and perceive the homespace, is to undermine the importance of both housing and home as key sites of political governance and control. The disconnection between studies of home and housing policy is an issue that this book has therefore sought to both highlight and redress.

## The current landscape

In this book I have traced the impacts of a range of punitive housing legislation over the course of the last decade. As previously highlighted, public interest and direct resistance to these policies has ebbed and waned.

However, at the time of writing, some legal headway has been made in reducing the impact of the bedroom tax. This has occurred on a variety of legal scales, as discussed in Chapter 5, from people using prior legal rulings to exempt themselves via the tribunal system, to Court of Appeal (2016) and Supreme Court (2019) rulings deeming the policy unlawful in some instances. This is certainly a step in the right direction for anti-bedroom tax campaigners. Social tenants seeking to challenge the policy have undoubtedly been greatly assisted by the fearless campaigning of the Carmichaels and others, as many will now be able to build a case for their own exemption eligibility based on these rulings. However, while it may have been weakened, the policy remains largely intact, and full repeal is highly unlikely to occur under a Conservative administration. Furthermore, while former leaders of the opposition Ed Miliband and Jeremy Corbyn were vocal in their promises to repeal the bedroom tax should Labour be elected, current leader (at the time of writing) Keir Starmer has been far quieter on the subject.

Family homelessness and a focus on temporary accommodation as its solution continues to run rampant in UK policymaking. However, since the COVID-19 pandemic hit in 2020, there has been increasing awareness of homelessness and housing inequality in the country. As Chapter 1 discussed, the pandemic brought into stark light government assumptions regarding the average British home (privately owned, comfortable, with spare bedrooms, multiple bathrooms and a garden), versus the realities of many people's home lives. In the same year, 23-year-old England footballer Marcus Rashford highlighted the extent of child poverty in Britain with his campaign to force a government U-turn on providing free school meals in school holidays during the pandemic. Rashford's tireless campaigning made explicit the plight of many families who, already on the financial edge before the pandemic, had been plunged into poverty in part as a consequence of spiking unemployment and losses in wages due to legal self-isolation requirements. The campaign also revealed the callousness of a government that had to be forced into providing such essential services for struggling families at a time of heightened uncertainty and precarity. As pandemic-based restrictions have come to an end, so too have these various hard-fought for support services, including eviction moratoriums and commitments to providing shelter for all homeless people. Rents in London have skyrocketed to an all-time high, and homelessness rates in the country have now surpassed pre-lockdown levels. Therefore, while public awareness of housing precarity has heightened, it remains a deeply entrenched issue.

There has been comparatively little public interest, either negative or positive, in the criminalisation of squatting since its introduction in 2012. This has proved to be something of a double-edged sword for squatters. On the one hand, there has been minimal political uptake in terms of repealing the law change, the most significant being an early day motion calling for repeal submitted by former Shadow Chancellor John McDonnell in 2013.

However, on the other, the political appetite for extending criminalisation to include commercial properties also appears to have waned, providing a limited saving grace for those who continue to squat in these highly precarious circumstances. Although shortly after the implementation of section 144 there were calls from across the political spectrum, including from prominent Labour politicians, to extend the law to include commercial properties (see Peck et al 2013), the impact of this was minimal, and the further criminalisation of squatting remains absent from current political discourse. This may in part be related to one of the most prominent anti-squatting politicians, Mike Weatherley, losing his seat to a Labour candidate in 2015 and resigning from public life due to illness. Although squatting remains a highly precarious form of homemaking, the lessening interest in extending its criminalisation does provide squatters with at least some respite from legal persecution. However, it appears extremely unlikely that section 144 will be repealed in the near future due to continued limited public sympathy for squatting as a practice.

## When crisis becomes the norm

This book has focused on the domicidal impacts of three London case studies. Clearly, repealing both the bedroom tax and section 144, and much greater regulation of the private rented sector would go a long way in re-establishing many people's access to home. These are clear end goals, and while I by no means wish to downplay the relief and return of agency that these changes would bring for many people in the capital and beyond, I nonetheless argue that such victories would be a treatment of the symptoms, rather than the cause. London is a city where the average house price is now over 12 times the average salary (Office for National Statistics 2020). A city where new housebuilding is usually marketed to investors before it is to Londoners themselves. A city whose poor are decanted from their homes and moved out of the capital in the name of 'regeneration'. A city where the poor that do remain are left to burn in their homes in one of the richest boroughs in the country, while wealthy Londoners look on from their luxury properties. What is needed is more than the repeal of policies such as section 144 and the bedroom tax, and the introduction of regulations such as rent caps. An entire rethink of what home means is essential if the gross inequalities present in the capital are ever to be redressed.

London is one of the epicentres of a near-global housing culture whereby almost all sense of housing-as-home, rather than financial investment, appears to have been lost. In major cities the world over, neoliberal governance has become the norm. This emphasis on the pursuit of individual wealth has seen average house prices far exceed average salaries, and commitment to state housebuilding decline. Homeownership has, since the 1970s in particular, been dogmatically encouraged as the apex of a successful home, and, to echo Margaret Thatcher, a successful nation. And yet, homeownership in the majority of Western, capitalist countries has drastically declined in recent decades as it becomes increasingly out of reach for even middle and higher earning groups (Arundel and Ronald 2021). More and more, housing is understood as a low-risk means of storing and accumulating wealth. Corporations and the uber-rich turn homes into mass profit both through landlordism and speculative investment – whereby housing purchased is left empty for as long as it takes to increase sufficiently in value before being sold on. This is a brutal decoupling of housing from home, and is stripping millions of people the world over of their rights to home. This process of hyper-financialisation is further aided by the demonisation of those whose homes are being taken away from them. Narratives that paint people as impoverished through their own making, or those attempting to live outside capitalist systems as innately criminal, underpin and legitimise housing as a tool for profit, and undermine home as foundational for human happiness. This is socio-symbolic domicide writ large. To return to the work of David Madden and Peter Marcuse, this is not the makings of a housing crisis, but rather the purposeful establishment of a new normal; one that legitimises the decimation of home for many for the purposes of profiting the few (Madden and Marcuse 2016). Gone are the days of an acute housing 'crisis' – we are now very much living in an era where, for many, domicide is the new normal.

## Final thoughts

While not ending on the most upbeat note, I do hope that this book can provide a springboard for further research that highlights working-class and low-income people's struggles in securing a right to home. In particular, greater focus on refugee and migrant Londoners' experiences of these issues is greatly needed (and something that has been beyond the scope of this book). I hope, too, that the book will encourage further action regarding the reintroduction of truly affordable housebuilding in London, particularly in terms of increasing the levels of social housing in a city that has become almost impossibly unaffordable even to those on middle incomes. Before this can happen, though, more housing solutions need to focus on the ways in which people's worth is so often defined by their housing tenure. One of the central arguments made in this book is that the power of political rhetoric, and the political potency of home, should not be underestimated. Until social tenants, low-income families, squatters and others who cannot, or do not wish to, access private homeownership are seen not as societal degenerates, but rather as people who have as much claim to home in London as anybody else, little will change. What is perhaps most daunting, though by no means insurmountable, is that for London's housing system to truly change, it is an entire national, or arguably international, attitude towards the home, and who is deserving of it, that needs to be addressed and restructured. Currently, signs that this is happening are limited. To return to Grenfell Tower, the fire that took so many lives and destroyed the homes of so many more brutally revealed the horrific and systemic inequalities that continue to be steadfast components of London's housing system (Madden 2017). Grenfell signifies multiple layers of domicide, where Kensington and Chelsea's decision to install flammable cladding is intrinsically connected to more long-term, embedded and violent decision-making regarding the low-income social tenants that often occupy post-war high-rises. The brutal reality is that the lives of those within Grenfell were ultimately not considered grievable enough to warrant protection from death. This is about more than a housing crisis: this is a crisis of humanity and sociability within our city, whereby social tenants, low-income families, squatters and others deemed to be unworthy are literally left to burn.

However, in the wake of such horrors there is hope that attitudes are beginning to change, with wider, global-scale campaigns emerging in recent years that demand a right to home be taken seriously. At the forefront of this is 'The Shift'. Established by Leilani Farha, former UN Special Rapporteur for adequate housing, The Shift is a global movement advocating universal decent housing through a human rights framework that centres the right to home. The Shift asks governments and other powerful actors to consciously reconceptualise the home as a human right, rather than a financial product. And in some cities, very public steps are being taken to reaffirm housing-as-home. For example, in September 2021, voters in Berlin resoundingly backed a referendum that demanded the local government buy hundreds of thousands of housing units from large property companies (Taylor 2021). While not legally binding, the vote has sent out a powerful message: that people are taking back their right to home. And to return to London, some tentative steps are being made to challenge the mass financialisation of housing. In July 2021 the Mayor of London Sadiq Khan introduced the 'Right to Buy Back' scheme, which gives local authorities the chance to bid for funding in order to buy back former council housing. As of August 2022, over 1,500 homes have been added to the capital's social housing stock through the scheme. While this is certainly a positive step in acknowledging the socioeconomic disparities that run rife in the capital and establishing solutions to social housing shortages, there remains a long road to reducing income gaps and the limitations lower-income Londoners face in terms of maintaining secure housing in the city. Unfortunately, what remains clear is that, despite the admirable intentions of Khan and some local authorities to address housing disparity in London, they ultimately have very little power, and are ideologically at odds with the national government. For example, the national Housing and Planning Act of 2016 extended the Right to Buy to include housing association properties, legislating for the sale of 'high-value' council properties to fund this extension. The Act also phased out secure tenancies for life for local authority tenants (Unison 2016). More recently still, in October 2021 Johnson's government cut Universal Credit (of which housing benefit is a component) by £20 per week. This is despite warnings from the charity Citizens Advice that the cut would lead to more than 2 million people ending up in debt. In short, though the future of housing and home in London is not devoid of hope, the reality is that those who lead the country continue to perpetuate the same narratives regarding who does and does not deserve a home.

In sum, the story told throughout this book is one of class disparity and the invasion of neoliberal logics into both our homes, and how we construct and categorise the homes of others. I have explored how the home has been dismantled, restructured and recontextualised for some of London's most precarious residents, as well as revealing the ways in which they respond to and challenge the domicide enacted upon them. In these chapters I have revealed the rhetorics of austerity pragmatism espoused by the Coalition and Conservative governments in the wake of recession to be a fallacy. Instead, austerity has been deployed as a means of moralising housing policy decisions and furthering constructions of particular groups as socially deviant, and therefore undeserving of home. I had hoped to end this book with a positive account of some clear structural shifts. And certainly, the ongoing and public legal challenges to the bedroom tax provide a particularly hopeful outcome of persistent resistive action. Jeremy Corbyn's surprising and positive result at the June 2017 general election also briefly invoked public desire for a shift towards a kinder, more inclusive politics that does not automatically deride people because of their housing circumstances. But ultimately, as long as financialisation is the centrepiece of the idealised home, policies and legislation will continue to dismantle the homemaking capacities of those seeking an alternative to neoliberal housing markets, and those who are unable to engage in the property market. In the meantime, we must keep fighting to ensure that London is, one day, a city that all, regardless of their socioeconomic status or housing choices, have the right to call home.

# Notes

## Introduction

[1] Although the bedroom tax also applies to Scotland and Northern Ireland, both devolved governments decided to cover the costs of the bedroom tax themselves. Squatting in all forms has been illegal in Scotland since 1865, and in Northern Ireland since 1946.

[2] Throughout the book, I refer to the criminalisation of squatting as 'section 144'.

[3] The role of neoliberalism as an ideology that perpetuates working-class domicide will be discussed more in Chapter 1. Broadly defined, neoliberalism refers to a political shift that began in the late 1970s/early 1980s that moved away from a focus on state-centric welfare and service provision, to a free market-led approach. Although some argue it is an overused term in academic work, neoliberalism remains a crucial mode of thinking and way of rationalising furthering inequality, not just in relation to housing but across all areas of society.

[4] Where requested, all participants have been anonymised.

[5] Snowballing refers to a recruitment method whereby an existing participant would suggest or introduce me to potential future interviewees.

## Chapter 1

[1] Domicide is, of course, far from solely a class-based process, and the ways in which class intersects across race, gender, sexuality and so on have profound implications for the forms and severity of domicide enacted. While in this book I do touch upon some of these intersections, namely in relation to the gendered stigmatisation of single mothers, a thorough investigation of the relationship between domicide and all forms of marginalisation is beyond the scope of this book.

[2] Although the right to buy had existed since the early 1970s, it was not until its inclusion in the 1980 Housing Act that the policy became widespread.

[3] At the time, the Aylesbury Estate in particular had come to symbolise the architectural and moral decay that is now so firmly associated with urban council estates.

[4] While council housing refers to housing built and managed by local authorities directly, the more modern 'social housing' incorporates the wider range of organisations involved in housing that sits outside of the private market, namely housing associations – which will be discussed further in Chapter 2. References to council housing are made throughout this book when I am talking solely about this original structure of state-managed housing.

[5] Section 21 of the Housing Act 1988 enables landlords to legally evict their tenants without reason as long as they provide at least a two-month notice period.

## Chapter 2

[1] The role of a newly emergent squatting movement in helping to push for the establishment of a mass council housebuilding project will be discussed in Chapter 4.

[2] More on how this links to the squatting movement of the same period in Chapter 4.

[3] Many of these concerns are akin to the issues with purpose-built temporary accommodation identified in Chapter 3.

[4] The shift in terminology here from council to social housing reflects the vast reduction in the role of local councils in housing provision, to a wider and more complex system.

[5] For example, some NHS trusts are spending as much as one-sixth of their budgets on debt repayments to PFIs (Campbell 2019).

[6] Margaret Thatcher introduced the officially titled 'Community Charge', in 1989 in Scotland and 1990 across England and Wales. The charge shifted taxation from one placed

on property, to a charge per head. The tax was widely criticised as placing the greatest burden on the working classes, and its implementation led to widespread rioting across the country.

7   In comparison, 19 per cent of the UK's working-age population have a disability.

8   A couple who needed to sleep in separate bedrooms due to Mrs Carmichael's spina bifida. This case and its impact will be discussed in more detail in Chapter 5.

9   Legally challenging the bedroom tax on discriminatory grounds has been an ongoing and prevalent part of the fight against the policy since its inception, and will be discussed in more detail in Chapter 5.

10   Discretionary Housing Payments are allocated to local authorities by central government to provide support for a range of housing costs and needs. They will be discussed in more detail in Chapter 5 in relation to their role in mitigating some of the effects of the bedroom tax.

11   Local Housing Allowance (LHA) is the name given to housing benefits for private renters. Prior to 2011, LHA rates were capped at the 50th percentile of properties for rent in a local area, essentially meaning that the cheapest 50 per cent of properties in an area would be covered by LHA. However, this changed in 2011, when the cap was reduced to the 30th percentile, meaning that only the cheapest 30 per cent of rental properties in an area would be covered by LHA, with tenants expected to make up the shortfall in rent themselves.

## Chapter 3

1   Some of this chapter is based on a report of PLACE/Ladywell written by myself and my colleagues in 2019 entitled *Temporary Homes, Permanent Progress? Resident Experiences of PLACE/Ladywell* (Harris, Brickell and Nowicki 2019).

2   The definition of intentional homelessness in England is set out in the Housing Act 1996. A person making a homeless application is intentionally homeless if all of the following apply:

- the applicant must deliberately have done, or failed to do, something in consequence of which they have ceased to occupy accommodation which was available to them;
- it must have been reasonable for the applicant to continue to occupy the accommodation;
- the applicant must have been aware of all the relevant facts before deliberately taking or failing to take the actions. An act or omission in good faith on the part of a person unaware of a relevant fact should not be treated as deliberate.

3   Royal Holloway, University of London.

4   Section 106 of the Town and Country Planning Act 1990 refers to legal agreements between local authorities and developers regarding measures that the developer must take to ensure a proposal is beneficial to the local area. This often involves commitments that certain percentages of residential developments are affordable housing.

## Chapter 4

1   The 'Homes Fit for Heroes' pledge refers in part to Minister of Health Dr Christopher Addison's 1919 Housing and Town Planning Act, seen as a defining legislative moment in which local councils were placed at the forefront of housing provision. The title of the pledge referred to a commitment to provide enough decent housing for those returning from the war.

2   This despite the fact that surveys undertaken by the Department of the Environment during the 1970s revealed that most squatted properties were in fact occupied by people with children (Platt 1999).

3   Adverse possession is a method of gaining legal ownership of rights to land or property from its previous owner, usually via a longstanding occupation of 12 years or more. This is usually what the term 'squatters' rights' refers to.

4   To date, section 144 of the Legal Aid, Sentencing and Punishment of Offenders Act criminalises squatting in residential buildings only. Squatting commercial buildings remains a civil, rather than criminal, offence.

5   The standard term for a squatter group.

6   An early day motion is a formal motion submitted for debate in the House of Commons, usually by an MP.

7   The subject of part of Chapter 5.

8   Although squatting in a commercial building remains a civil, rather than criminal, offence and is not subject to the same risk of fining and/or imprisonment, all of the squatters that I spoke with told me that there had also been a crackdown on commercial squat evictions since the implementation of section 144.

9   To be revisited in Chapter 5.

10  Although it has been known for notice to be as little as 48 hours.

11  Unlike squatters, property guardians tend to have middling incomes. They tend to be young professionals, particularly those working in creative industries. For a more detailed discussion of guardian demographics, see Ferreri et al (2017).

12  Although, Dave, Tariq and Matteo found an ingenious means of tapping into this very same aesthetic in order to help protect their home, as will be discussed in the next chapter.

## Chapter 5

1   First- and Upper-tier Tribunals form part of the 2007 overhaul of the tribunal system in the UK. First-tier Tribunals are divided into seven chambers, structured around subject areas. There are four Upper-tier Tribunals, where decisions made in First-tier Tribunals can be appealed.

2   The loophole was helpful but short-lived, with the Department for Work and Pensions closing it in 2014.

3   DSS refers to the now-defunct Department of Social Security. 'No DSS' is a term commonly used by private landlords and letting agents, denoting that they will not rent properties to people in receipt of housing benefit.

4   The Greater London Council (GLC) was the top administrative body for Greater London from 1965 until 1986, when it was disbanded by the Thatcher government. The body was re-established as the Greater London Authority (GLA) in 2000.

# References

Aalbers, M. 2016. *The Financialization of Housing: A political economy approach.* London: Routledge.

Amara, P. 2014. E15 'occupation': We shall not be moved, say Stratford single parents fighting eviction after occupying empty homes. *The Independent.* Accessed online: http://www.independent.co.uk/news/uk/home-news/ e15-occupation- we-shall-not-be-moved-say-stratford-single-parents- fighting-eviction- after-occupying-9761186.html

Arundel, R. and Ronald, R. 2021. The false promises of homeownership: Homeowner societies in an era of declining access and rising inequality, *Urban Studies* 58(6): 1120–1140.

Atkinson, R. and Jacobs, K. 2016. *House, Home and Society.* London: Palgrave Macmillan.

Bailey, R. 1973. *The Squatters.* Harmondsworth: Penguin.

Barker, N. 2020. The housing pandemic: Four graphs showing the link between COVID-19 deaths and the housing crisis. *Inside Housing.* Available online: Inside Housing – Insight – The housing pandemic: four graphs showing the link between COVID-19 deaths and the housing crisis

Baxter, D. and Brickell, K. 2014. For home unmaking, *Home Cultures* 11(2):133–143.

BBC. 2010. *Do the poor have a right to live in expensive areas?* Accessed online: http://www.bbc.co.uk/news/magazine-11674864

BBC. 2013. *Grow Heathrow: Campaigners rejected by Court of Appeal.* Accessed online: http://www.bbc.co.uk/news/uk-england-london-23155782

BBC. 2015. *David Cameron on family life in the Cotswolds.* Accessed online: http://www.bbc.co.uk/news/uk-politics-32025336

BBC. 2016. *'Bedroom tax': Government loses Court of Appeal cases.* Accessed online: http://www.bbc.co.uk/news/uk-35418488

BBC. 2021. *Grenfell Tower survivors say criminal charges are taking too long.* Accessed online: https://www.bbc.co.uk/news/uk-england-london- 59657356

Bentley, H. 2008. Council homes: The rise, the collapse and the fall. *The Guardian.* Accessed online: http://www.theguardian.com/society/2008/ aug/13/communities.hou sing

Berlant, L. 2011. *Cruel Optimism.* Durham, NC: Duke University Press.

Blair, T. 1997. *Speech at the Aylesbury Estate, 2 June.* Available online: https:// www.youtube.com/watch?v=q_HGgT--AGs

Blandy, S. and Hunter, C. 2013. The Right to Buy: Examination of an exercise in allocating, shifting and re-branding risks, *Critical Social Policy* 33(1): 17–36.

Blunden, M., Davenport, J. and Kitson, R. 2013. Squatters take over Britain's most expensive council house on same day Southwark sold it for £3m. *Evening Standard*. Accessed online: http://www.standard.co.uk/news/london/squatters-take-over-britains-most-expensive-council-house-on-same-day-southwark-sold-it-for-3m-8910772.html

Blunt, A. 2005. Cultural geography: Cultural geographies of home, *Progress in Human Geography* 29(4): 505–515.

Blunt, A. and Dowling, R. 2006. *Home*. Oxon: Routledge.

Blunt, A. and Varley, A. 2004. Geographies of home, *cultural geographies* 11(1): 3–6.

Bourquin, P., Joyce, R. and Keiller, A. 2020. Living standards, poverty and inequality in the UK: 2020. *Institute for Fiscal Studies*. Accessed online: https://ifs.org.uk/publications/living-standards-poverty-and-inequality-uk-2020

Bramall, R. 2013. *The Cultural Politics of Austerity: Past and present in austere times*. London: Palgrave Macmillan.

Brickell, K. 2012a. Geopolitics of Home, *Geography Compass* 6(10): 575–588.

Brickell, K. 2012b. 'Mapping' and 'doing' critical geographies of home. *Progress in Human Geography* 36(2): 225–244.

Brickell, K. 2014. 'The whole world is watching': Intimate geopolitics of forced eviction and women's activism in Cambodia, *Annals of the Association of American Geographers* 104(6): 1256–1272.

Brickell, K., Fernandez Arrigoitia, M. and Vasudevan, A. (eds). 2017. *Geographies of Forced Eviction: Dispossession, violence, resistance*. London: Palgrave Macmillan.

Brown, C. 2013a. Cameron: Bedroom tax is not a tax. *Inside Housing*. Accessed online: http://www.insidehousing.co.uk/tenancies/cameron-bedroom-tax-is-not-a-tax/6525647.article

Brown, C. 2013b. Peer defends 'bedroom tax' term. *Inside Housing*. Accessed online: http://www.insidehousing.co.uk/peer-defends-bedroom-tax-term/6526030.article

Brown, R. 2021. A group of renters just won £19,000 from their billionaire landlord – and they're just getting started. Novara Media. Accessed online: https://novaramedia.com/2021/07/23/a-group-of-renters-just-won-19000-from-their-billionaire-landlord-and-theyre-just-getting-started/

Burrell, K. 2014. Spilling over from the street: Contextualising domestic space in an inner-city neighbourhood, *Home Cultures* 11(2): 145–166.

Butler, J. 2009. *Frames of War*. London: Verso.

Caldeira, T. 2001. *City of Walls: Crime, segregation and citizenship in São Paulo*. Berkeley and Los Angeles: University of California Press.

Calder, A. 1969. *The People's War: Britain 1939–1945*. London: Pimlico.

Camelot Europe. 2015. *Property guardianship: how it works*. Accessed online: http://uk.cameloteurope.com/9/0/how-it-works/property-guard ianship-how-it-works.html

Cameron, D. 2009. *Age of austerity speech*. Conservative Party Speeches. Accessed online: http://conservative-speeches.sayit.mysociety.org/speech/601367

Cameron, D. 2011a. *PM's speech on Welfare Reform Bill*. Available online: https://www.gov.uk/government/speeches/pms-speech-on-welfare-reform-bill

Cameron, D. 2011b. *Troubled families speech*. Cabinet Office.

Cameron, D. 2014. *Speech to Conservative Party Conference*. Available online: http://press.conservatives.com/post/98882674910/david-came ron-speech-to-conservative-party

Cameron, D. 2015. *PM speech on opportunity*. Accessed online: https://www.gov.uk/government/speeches/pm-speech-on-opportunity

Campbell, D. 2019. NHS hospital trusts to pay out further £55bn under PFI scheme. *The Guardian*. Accessed online: https://www.theguardian.com/politics/2019/sep/12/nhs-hospital-trusts-to-pay-out-further-55bn-under-pfi-scheme

Campkin, B. 2013. *Remaking London: Decline and regeneration in urban culture*. London: I.B. Tauris & Co.

Chakrabortty, A. 2017. Over 170 years after Engels, Britain is still a country that murders its poor. *The Guardian*. Accessed online: https://www.theguardian.com/commentisfree/2017/jun/20/engels-britain-murders-poor-grenfell-tower

Chapman, J. 2013. A Marxist diatribe! Ministers' fury as 'Brazil nut' UN inspector who lectured Britain publishes report condemning our housing benefit. *Daily Mail*. Accessed online: Ministers condemn 'Brazil nut' UN inspector | Daily Mail Online

Chorley, M. 2013. United Nations disown the 'loopy Brazilian leftie' official who came to Britain and demanded the bedroom tax be axed. *Daily Mail*. Accessed online: United Nations disown the 'loopy Brazilian leftie' official who came to Britain and demanded the bedroom tax be axed | Daily Mail Online

Clarke, J. and Newman, J. 2012. The alchemy of austerity, *Critical Social Policy* 32(3): 299–319.

Coates, H. 2016. Shared care and the bedroom tax: Can housing and family law be reconciled? *Becket Chambers*. Accessed online: http://becket-chamb ers.co.uk/2016/01/22/shared-care-and-the-bedroom-tax-can-housing-and-family-law-be-reconciled/

Cobb, N. and Fox, L. 2007. Living outside the system? The (im)morality of urban squatting after the Land Registration Act 2002, *Legal Studies* 27(2): 236–260.

Cresswell, T. 2010. Mobilities I, *Progress in Human Geography* 35(4): 550–558.

Crossley, S. and Slater, T. 2014. Benefits Street: Territorial stigmatization and the realization of a 'television of divisions', *Values & Value.* ESRC & Goldsmiths.

Csikzentmihalyi, M. and Rochberg-Halton, E. 1981. *The Meaning of Things: Domestic symbols and the self.* Cambridge: Cambridge University Press.

Dangerfield, A. 2012. Grow Heathrow: Green-fingered squatters' eviction fight. *BBC News.* Accessed online: http://www.bbc.co.uk/news/uk-england-london-18460865

Darling, J. 2011. Domopolitics, governmentality and the regulation of asylum accommodation', *Political Geography* 30: 263–271.

Delaney, D. 2004. Tracing displacements: Or evictions in the nomosphere, *Environment and Planning D: Society and Space* 22(6): 847–860.

Delaney, D. 2016. Legal geography II: Discerning injustice, *Progress in Human Geography* 40(2): 267–274

Department for Levelling Up, Housing and Communities. 2022. *Levelling up the United Kingdom.* Accessed online: https://www.gov.uk/government/publications/levelling-up-the-united-kingdom

Department for Work and Pensions. 2013. *Local authorities and advisers: removal of the spare room subsidy.* Accessed online: https://www.gov.uk/government/collections/local-authorities-removal-of-the-spare-room-subsidy

Department for Work and Pensions. 2014. *Simplifying the welfare system and making sure work pays.* Accessed online: https://www.gov.uk/government/publications/2010-to-2015-government-policy-welfare-reform/2010-to-2015-government-policy-welfare-reform

Department for Work and Pensions. 2015. *Housing Benefit caseload statistics: data to February 2015.* Accessed online: https://www.gov.uk/government/statistics/housing-benefit-caseload-statistics

DeWard, S. and Moe, A. 2010. 'Like a prison!' Homeless women's narratives of surviving shelter, *Journal of Society and Social Welfare* 37: 115.

Domosh, M. 1998. Geography and gender: Home, again? *Progress in Human Geography* 22(2): 276–282.

Dorling, D. 2011. *Injustice: Why social inequality persists.* Bristol: The Policy Press.

Dorling, D. 2014. *All That Is Solid: How the great housing disaster defines our times, and what we can do about it.* London: Allen Lane.

Doughty, S. 2013. £300-a-night hotel for the Brazilian United Nations inspector who lectured Britain over 'bedroom tax', *Daily Mail.* Accessed online: UN Inspector Raquel Rolnik stayed in £300-per-night hotel | Daily Mail Online

Dovey, K. 1985. Home and homelessness, in Altman, I. and Werner, C. M (eds), *Home Environments.* New York and London: Plenum Press, pp 33–64.

Dubuis, A. 2014. Empty council estate occupation by young mothers made homeless after hostel closure slammed by Newham councillors. *Evening Standard*. Accessed online: http://www.standard.co.uk/news/london/empty-council-estate-occupation-by-young-mothers-made-homeless-after-hostel-closure-slammed-by-9752281.html

Enloe, C. 2011. The mundane matters, *International Political Sociology* 5(4): 447–450.

*Evening Standard*. 2011. *Squatters say 'sorry' and finally leave pregnant woman's home*. Accessed online: http://www.standard.co.uk/news/squatters-say-sorry-and-finally- leave-pregnant-womans-home-6440970.html

Fernandez, R. and Aalbers, M. 2016. Financialization and housing: Between globalisation and varieties of capitalism, *Competition and Change* 20(2): 71–88.

Ferreri, M. and Dawson, G. 2018. Self-precaritization and the spatial imaginaries of property guardianship, *cultural geographies* 25(3): 425–440.

Ferreri, M., Dawson, G. and Vasudevan, A. 2017. Living precariously: Property guardianship and the flexible city, *Transactions of the Institute of British Geographers* 42(2): 246–259.

Fiaz, R. 2018. focuse15.org. Accessed online: https://focuse15.org/2018/07/31/a-victory-in-court-but-thefight-against-intentional-homelessness-goes-on/

Finchett-Maddock, L. 2014. Squatting in London: Squatters' rights and legal movement(s), in van der Steen, B., Katzeff, A. and van Hoogenhuijze, L. (eds), *The City Is Ours: Squatting and autonomous movements in Europe from the 1970s to the present*. Oakland, CA: PM Press, pp 207–232.

Flint, J. 2003. Housing and ethopolitics: Constructing identities of active consumption and responsible community, *Economy and Society* 32(3): 611–629.

Floyd, J. 2004. Coming out of the kitchen: Texts, contexts and debates, *cultural geographies* 11(1): 61–73.

Foot, M. 1973. *Aneurin Bevan: A biography, Vol. II 1945–1960*. London: Faber and Faber.

Forrest, M. 2017. Engaging and disrupting power: The public value of political ethnography, *Political Science & Politics* 50(1): 109–113.

Foucault, M. 1991. Governmentality, in Burchell, G. (ed), *The Foucault Effect: Studies in governmentality*. Chicago: University of Chicago Press, pp 87–104.

Gerbaudo, P. 2012. *Tweets and the Streets: Social media and contemporary activism*. London: Pluto.

Giddens, A. 1990. *The Consequences of Modernity*. Cambridge: Polity.

Gilbert, D. and Preston, R. 2003. 'Stop being so English': Suburban modernity and national identity in the twentieth century, in Gilbert, D., Matless, D. and Short, B. (eds), *Geographies of British Modernity: Space and society in the twentieth century*. Malden, MA, Oxford and Victoria: Blackwell Publishing, pp 185–203.

Government Land Registry. 2016. *House Price Index Monthly Report: March 2016*.

Grenfell United. No date. Accessed online: https://grenfellunited.org.uk/ our-story

Hall, R. 2021. One in four Londoners in temporary housing outside their local area. *The Guardian*. Accessed online: https://www.theguardian.com/ society/2021/jun/02/one-in-four-londoners-in-temporary-housing-outs ide-their-local-area?CMP=Share_AndroidApp_Other

Hanley, L. 2007. *Estates: An intimate history*. London: Granta Publications.

Harker, C. 2009. Spacing Palestine through the home, *Transactions of the Institute of British Geographers* 34(3): 320–332.

Harker, C. 2012. Precariousness, precarity and family: Notes from Palestine, *Environment and Planning A* 44(4): 849–865.

Harris, A. 2012. Art and gentrification: Pursuing the urban pastoral in Hoxton, London, *Transactions of the Institute of British Geographers* 37(2): 226–241.

Harris, E. 2015. Navigating pop-up geographies: Urban space-times of flexibility, interstitiality and immersion, *Geography Compass* 9(11): 592–603.

Harris, E. 2020. *Rebranding Precarity: Pop-up culture as the seductive new normal*. London: Bloomsbury Publishing.

Harris, E. and Nowicki, M. 2018. Cultural geographies of precarity, *cultural geographies* 25(3): 387–391.

Harris, E., Brickell, K. and Nowicki, M. 2019. *Temporary Homes, Permanent Progress? Resident Experiences of PLACE/Ladywell*. Royal Holloway, University of London. Accessed online: https://pure.royalholloway. ac.uk/ws/portalfiles/portal/34520821/LewishamReport_FINAL_Sep_ 2019.pdf

Harris, E., Brickell, K. and Nowicki, M. 2020. Door locks, wall stickers, fireplaces: Assemblage theory and home (un)making in Lewisham's temporary accommodation, *Antipode* 52(5): 1286–1309.

Harris, E., Nowicki, M. and Brickell, K. 2019. On-edge in the impasse: Inhabiting the housing crisis as structure-of-feeling, *Geoforum* 101: 156–164.

Hartley, E. and Atherton, B. 2016. Sisters Uncut 'reclaim' empty council home and transform it into community centre. *Huffpost*. Accessed online: https://www.huffingtonpost.co.uk/entry/sisters-uncut-occupy-council-house-in-hackney-to-fight-gentrification_uk_57838055e4b09 35d4b4b2a76

Heath, L. 2021. Four graphs showing the state of homelessness in England, *Inside Housing*. Accessed online: https://www.insidehousing.co.uk/insight/ insight/four-graphs-showing-the-state-of-homelessness-in-england-69442

Hirsch, D. 2021. The cost of child poverty in 2021. *Centre for Research in Social Policy: Loughborough University*. Accessed online: https://www.lboro.ac.uk/media/wwwlboroacuk/content/crsp/downloads/reports/The%20Cost%20of%20Child%20Poverty%20in%202021_CRSP%20Paper.pdf

HM Treasury. 2015. *Summer Budget 2015: Key announcements*. Accessed online: https://www.gov.uk/government/news/summer-budget-2015-key-announcements

Hodkinson, S. 2011. The Private Finance Initiative in English council housing regeneration: A privatisation too far?, *Housing Studies* 26(6): 911–932.

Hodkinson, S. 2012. The return of the housing question. *Ephemera: Theory & Politics in Organisation* 12(4): 423–444.

Hodkinson, S. and Essen, C. 2015. Grounding accumulation by dispossession in everyday life: The unjust geographies of urban regeneration under the Private Finance Initiative, *International Journal of Law in the Built Environment* 7(1): 72–91.

Hodkinson, S. and Robbins, G. 2013. The return of class war conservatism? Housing under the UK Coalition Government, *Critical Social Policy* 33(1): 57–77.

Hopkin Murray Beskine. 2020. *Grand Chamber of European Court of Human Rights Rules Against the United Kingdom in Gender Violence 'Bedroom Tax' Case*. Accessed online: http://www.hmbsolicitors.co.uk/news/category/item/index.cfm?asset_id=1751

House of Brag. 2014. *The London Queer Social Centre*. Accessed online: https://houseofbrag.wordpress.com/about/

Hynek, N. 2012. The domopolitics of Japanese human security, *Security Dialogue* 43(2): 119–137.

Imrie, R. 2014. Space, place and policy regimes: The changing contours of disability and citizenship, in Soldatic, K., Roulstone, A. and Morgan, H. (eds), *Disability, Spaces and Places of Policy Exclusion*. London: Routledge, pp 13–30.

Jayanetti, C. 2021. Cut of £40m in help for tenants will 'drive up homelessness'. *The Guardian*. Accessed online: https://www.theguardian.com/money/2021/jun/06/cut-of-40m-in-help-for-tenants-will-drive-up-homelessness

Jones, R. 2018. As small as 13 sq metres: are these the worst new flats in Britain? *The Guardian*. Accessed online: https://www.theguardian.com/money/2018/aug/25/flats-block-converting-offices-living-space

Joseph Rowntree Foundation. 2017. *100 families a day lose their homes after evictions reach record high*. Accessed online: https://www.jrf.org.uk/press/100-families-day-lose-their-homes

Kallin, H. 2011. *Rethinking Regeneration in the PARC: Demolition, stock-transfer and consultation on Edinburgh's fringe*. PhD thesis: University of Edinburgh.

Kallin, H. and Slater, T. 2014. Activating territorial stigma: Gentrifying marginality on Edinburgh's periphery, *Environment and Planning A* 46(6): 1351–1368.

Katz, C. 2004. *Growing Up Global: Economic restructuring and children's everyday lives*. Minneapolis: University of Minnesota Press.

Laville, S. 2017. Grow Heathrow runway protest community given 14 days to leave site. *The Guardian*. Accessed online: https://www.theguardian.com/environment/2017/jun/29/grow-heathrow-runway-protest-community-given-14-days-to-leave-site

Lees, L. 2000. A reappraisal of gentrification: Towards a 'geography of gentrification', *Progress in Human Geography* 24(3): 389–408.

Lees, L. 2014. The urban injustices of New Labour's 'New Urban Renewal': The case of the Aylesbury Estate in London, *Antipode* 46(4): 921–947.

Lees, L. and Ferreri, M. 2016. Resisting gentrification on its final frontiers: Learning from the Heygate Estate in London (1974–2013), *Cities* 57: 14–24.

Lees, L., Slater, T. and Wyly, E. 2013. *Gentrification*. London: Routledge.

Lefebvre, H. 2014. *Critique of Everyday Life*. London: Verso.

Leigh Day. 2014. *Bedroom tax housing benefit appeal victory*. Accessed online: https://www.leighday.co.uk/News/2014/April-2014/Bedroom-Tax,-housing-benefit-appeal-victory

Leigh Day. 2019. *Man wins Supreme Court bedroom tax case*. Accessed online: https://www.leighday.co.uk/latest-updates/news/2019-news/man-wins-supreme-court-bedroom-tax-case/

Lewisham Mayor and Cabinet. 2021. *The Future of PLACE/Ladywell*. Accessed online: https://councilmeetings.lewisham.gov.uk/documents/s76839/Future%20of%20PLACE%20Ladywell.pdf

Lewisham Poverty Commission. 2017. *Lewisham Poverty Commission 2nd Meeting, 4th May 2017, Housing*, London: Lewisham Poverty Commission.

Light, A. 1991. *Forever England: Femininity, literature and conservatism between the wars*. Oxon, New York: Routledge.

Llewellyn, M. 2004. Designed by women and designing women: Gender, planning and the geographies of the kitchen in Britain 1917–1946. *Cultural Geographies* 11(1): 42–60.

Lowe, S., Searle, B. and Smith, S. 2012. From housing wealth to mortgage debt: The emergence of Britain's asset-shaped welfare state, *Social Policy and Society* 11(1): 105–116.

Machin, D. and Mayr, A. 2012. *How to Do Critical Discourse Analysis*. London: SAGE Publications.

Madden, D. 2017. Deadly Cityscapes of Inequality, *The Sociological Review*. Available online: https://thesociologicalreview.org/collection/urban-sociologies/deadly-cityscapes-of-inequality/

Madden, D. and Marcuse, P. 2016. *In Defense of Housing*. London, New York: Verso.

Manzo, L. 2003. Beyond house and haven: Toward a revisioning of emotional relationships with places, *Journal of Environmental Psychology* 23(1): 47–61.

Middleton, T. 2015. The role of rhetoric in the criminalisation of squatting, in Fox O'Mahony, L., O'Mahoney, D. and Hickey, R. (eds), *Moral Rhetoric and the Criminalisation of Squatting: Vulnerable demons?* Oxon: Routledge, pp 87–109.

Miller, D. 2001. *Home Possessions: Material culture behind closed doors*. London: Bloomsbury Academic.

Miller, D. 2008. *The Comfort of Things*. London: Polity.

Ministry of Justice. 2011. *Advice on dealing with squatters in your home*. Accessed online: https://assets.publishing.service.gov.uk/government/uploads/system/uploads/attachment_data/file/187348/squatters.pdf

Ministry of Justice. 2012. Circular No. 2012/04, *Offence of Squatting in a Residential Building*. Accessed online: https://assets.publishing.service.gov.uk/government/uploads/system/uploads/attachment_data/file/220062/squatting-circular.pdf

Minton, A. 2017. *Big Capital: Who is London for?* New York: Penguin Books.

Mitchell, D. 2003. *The Right to the City: Social justice and the fight for public space*. New York, London: Guilford Press.

Mitchell, D. T. and Snyder, S. L. 2015. *The Biopolitics of Disability: Neoliberalism, ablenationalism and peripheral embodiment*. Michigan: University of Michigan Press.

Moffatt, S., Lawson, S., Patterson, R., Holding, E., Dennison, A., Sowden, S. and Brown, J. 2016. A qualitative study of the impact of the UK 'bedroom tax', *Journal of Public Health* 38(2): 197–205.

Morley, D. 2003. What's 'home' got to do with it? Contradictory dynamics in the domestication of technology and the dislocation of domesticity, *Cultural Studies* 6: 435–458.

Mullins, D. 2010. Housing Associations. *Third Sector Research Centre Working Paper 16*. Accessed online: https://www.birmingham.ac.uk/Documents/college-social-sciences/social-policy/tsrc/working-papers/briefing-paper-16.pdf

Nixon, R. 2013. *Slow Violence and the Environmentalism of the Poor*. Harvard: Harvard University Press.

Norwood, G. 2010. Property guardian schemes offer quirky homes at low rents. But not for long. *The Guardian*. Accessed online: http://www.theguardian.com/money/2010/jan/10/property-guardian-schemes

Nowicki, M. 2014. Rethinking domicide: Towards an expanded critical geography of home, *Geography Compass* 8(11): 785–795.

Nowicki, M. 2017. Domicide and the Coalition: Austerity, citizenship and moralities of forced eviction in Inner London, in Brickell, K., Fernandez, M. and Vasudevan, A. (eds), *Geographies of Forced Eviction: Dispossession, violence, resistance*. London: Palgrave Macmillan, pp 121–143.

Nowicki, M. 2018. A Britain that everyone is proud to call home? The Conservative Party and rhetorics of homemaking and *un*making, *Social & Cultural Geography* 19(5): 647–667.

Nowicki, M. 2021. Is anyone home? Appropriating and re-narrativising London's post-criminalisation squatting scene, *Environment and Planning C: Politics and Space* 39(4): 838–855.

Nowicki, M., Brickell, K. and Harris, E. 2019. The hotelisation of the housing crisis: Experiences of family homelessness in Dublin hotels, *The Geographical Journal* 183(3) 313–324.

Office for National Statistics. 2018. *UK private rented sector: 2018.* Accessed online: https://www.ons.gov.uk/economy/inflationandpriceindices/articles/ukprivaterentedsector/2018

Office for National Statistics. 2020. *Private rental market summary statistics in England: October 2019 to September 2020.* Accessed online: https://www.ons.gov.uk/peoplepopulationandcommunity/housing/bulletins/privaterentalmarketsummarystatisticsinengland/october2019toseptember2020

Office for National Statistics. 2022. *UK House Price Index: April 2022.* Accessed online: https://www.ons.gov.uk/economy/inflationandpriceindices/bulletins/housepriceindex/april2022#house-prices-by-region

Osborne, H. and Norris, S. 2016. Pop-up village in south-east London to house homeless families. *The Guardian.* Accessed online: https://www.theguardian.com/society/2016/mar/18/pop-up-village-in-south-east-london-to-house-homeless-families

Oswin, N. 2010. Sexual tensions in modernizing Singapore: The postcolonial and the intimate, *Environment and Planning D* 28(1): 128–141.

Ó Tuathail, G. and Dahlman, C. 2006. Post-domicide Bosnia and Herzegovina: Homes, homelands and one million returns, *International Peacekeeping* 13(2): 242–260.

Pawson, H. and Mullins, D. 2010. *After Council Housing: Britain's new social landlords.* Basingstoke: Palgrave Macmillan.

Peck, J. and Tickell, A. 2002. Neoliberalizing space, *Antipode* 34(3): 380–404.

Peck, L., Jowell, T. and Umuna, C. 2013. *Squatting on commercial property.* Accessed online: http://lambethnews.files.wordpress.com/2013/09/fao-chris-grayling- mp.pdf

Perkins, A. 2013. The bedroom tax: Echoes of the poll tax. *The Guardian.* Accessed online: http://www.theguardian.com/society/2013/sep/24/bedroom-tax- echoes-poll-tax

Piacentini, T. 2016. Refugee solidarity in the everyday, *Soundings: A Political Journal of Politics and Culture* 64: 57–61.

Platt, S. 1999. Home truths: Media representations of homelessness, in Franklin, B. (ed), *Social Policy, the Media and Misrepresentation*. London: Routledge, pp 104–117.

PoliticsHome. 2018. *READ IN FULL: Theresa May's speech to the 2018 Conservative Party conference*. Accessed online: https://www.politicshome.com/news/article/read-in-full-theresa-mays-speech-to-the-2018-conservative-party-conference

Porteous, J. and Smith, S. 2001. *Domicide: The global destruction of home.* Montreal & Kingston: McGill-Queens University Press.

Precey, M., Sturdy, J. and Cawley, L. 2019. Inside Harlow's office block 'human warehouse' housing. *BBC*. Accessed online: https://www.bbc.co.uk/news/uk-england-essex-47720887

Pruijt, H. 2013. The logic of urban squatting, *International Journal of Urban and Regional Research* 37(1): 19–45.

Radley, A., Hodgetts, D. and Cullen, A. 2006. Fear, romance and transience in the lives of homeless women, *Social & Cultural Geography* 7(3): 347–461.

Ravetz, A. 2001. *Council Housing and Culture: The history of a social experiment.* London: Routledge.

Reeve, K. 2011. Squatting: A homelessness issue. *Crisis.* Accessed online: http://www.crisis.org.uk/data/files/publications/Crisis_Squatting Report_SEP T2011.pdf

Reeve, K. 2015. Criminalising the poor: Squatting, homelessness, and social welfare, in Fox O'Mahony, L., O'Mahoney, D. and Hickey, R. (eds), *Moral Rhetoric and the Criminalisation of Squatting: Vulnerable demons?* London, Oxon: Routledge, pp 133–154.

Relph, E. 1976. *Places and Placelessness.* London: Pion.

Reynolds, L. and Dzalto, A. 2019. Generation Homeless: The numbers behind the story. *Shelter.* Accessed online: https://england.shelter.org.uk/professional_resources/policy_and_research/policy_library/generation_homeless_the_numbers_behind_the_story

Richardson, H. 2020. 'No DSS' letting bans 'ruled unlawful' by court. *BBC.* Accessed online: https://www.bbc.co.uk/news/education-53391516

Roberts, R. 2017. Grenfell Tower blogger threatened with legal action by council after writing about safety concerns. *The Independent.* Accessed online: http://www.independent.co.uk/news/uk/home-news/grenfell-tower-fire-blogger-threatened-legal-action-kensington-and-chelsea-council-health-safety-a7792346.html

Robinson, R. 1995. The racial limits of the Fair Housing Act: The intersection of dominant white images, the violence of neighborhood purity, and the master narrative of black inferiority, *William and Mary Law Review* 37(1): 71–159.

Rolnik, R. 2003. Late neoliberalism: The financialization of homeownership and housing rights, *International Journal of Urban and Regional Research* 37(3): 1058–1066.

Rolnik, R. 2013. Report of the Special Rapporteur on adequate housing as component of the right to an adequate standard of living, and on the right to non-discrimination in this context, *United Nations General Assembly: Human Rights Council*. Accessed online: https://digitallibrary.un.org/record/766905?ln=en

Ryan, F. 2019. The bedroom tax is still ruining lives. Its victims need to know they matter. *The Guardian*. Accessed online: https://www.theguardian.com/commentisfree/2019/oct/31/bedroom-tax-victims-forgotten-welfare-reform

Ryan, F. 2020. *Crippled: Austerity and the demonization of disabled people.* London, New York: Verso.

Rybczynski, W. 1988. *Home: A short history of an idea.* London: Heinemann.

Sagoe, C. 2019. Permitted development scandal: Homeless families put at risk. *Shelter blog.* Accessed online: https://blog.shelter.org.uk/2019/04/permitted-development-scandal-homeless-families-put-at-risk/

Saunders, P. 1988. *A Nation of Home-owners.* London: Unwin Hyman.

Schatz, E. 2009. Ethnographic immersion and the study of politics, in Schatz, E. (ed), *Political Ethnography: What immersion contributes to the study of power.* Chicago: University of Chicago Press, pp 1–23.

Shapps, G. 2013. *Letter to United Nations General Secretary Ban Ki-Moon.* Accessed online: http://www.scribd.com/doc/167313006/MoonBanki.

Sibley, D. 1995. *Geographies of Exclusion: Society and difference in the West.* London, New York: Routledge.

Sisson, A. 2020. Territory and territorial stigmatisation: On the production, consequences and contestation of spatial disrepute, Progress in Human Geography 45(4): 659–681.

Slater, T. 2013. Expulsions from public housing: The hidden context of concentrated affluence, *Cities* 35: 384–390.

Slater, T. 2016a. Revanchism, stigma, and the production of ignorance: Housing struggles in austerity Britain, in Soederberg, S. (ed), *Risking Capitalism: Research in political economy Volume 31*, Bingley, UK: Emerald Group, pp 23–48.

Slater, T. 2016b. *From territorial stigma to territorial justice: a critique of vested interest urbanism*, 13th David M. Smith Annual Lecture, Queen Mary, University of London.

Slater, T. 2018. The invention of the 'sink estate': Consequential categorization and the UK housing crisis, *The Sociological Review* 66(4): 877–897.

Slater, T. and Anderson, N. 2012. The reputational ghetto: Territorial stigmatisation in St Paul's, Bristol, *Transactions of the Institute of British Geographers* 37(4): 530–546.

Smith, S. 2008. Owner-occupation: At home with a hybrid of money and materials, *Environment and Planning A* 40(3): 520–535.

Smith, S. 2011. Home price dynamics: A behavioural economy?, *Housing, Theory and Society* 28(3): 236–261.

Smith, S. 2014. Intimacy and angst in the field, *Gender, Place & Culture* 23(1): 134–146.

Somerville, P. 1992. Homelessness and the meaning of home: Rooflessness or rootlessness? *International Journal of Urban and Regional Research* 16(4): 529–539.

Spencer, R., Reeve-Lewis, B., Rugg, J. and Barata, E. 2020. Journeys in the shadow private rented sector, Report, Cambridge House, University of York.

SQUASH (Squatter's Action for Secure Homes). 2011. *Criminalising the vulnerable: Why we can't criminalise our way out of a housing crisis: A parliamentary briefing 18 May 2011.* Accessed online: http://www.squashcampaign.org/docs/SQUASH-Criminalising_The_Vulnerable-May2011.pdf

SQUASH. 2013. *The case against section 144.* Accessed online: http://www.squashcampaign.org/repeal-law/the-case-against-section-144-2/

Standing, G. 2011. *The Precariat: The new dangerous class.* London, New York: Bloomsbury Academic.

Sunak, R. 2021. *Autumn Budget and Spending Review 2021 Speech.* Accessed online: https://www.gov.uk/government/speeches/autumn-budget-and-spending-review-2021-speech

Taylor, A. 2021. Berlin voters asked the city to tackle rising rents. The plan is a long shot, but the message is powerful. *The Washington Post.* Accessed online: https://www.washingtonpost.com/world/2021/09/29/germany-berlin-rent-referendum/

Terkenli, T. 1995. Home as a region, *Geographical Review* 85(3): 324–334.

Thatcher, M. 1987. Interview for Woman's Own. *Margaret Thatcher Foundation.* Available online: http://www.margaretthatcher.org/document/106689

*The Daily Mail.* 2011a. *Victory over the squatters: Doctor and his heavily pregnant wife celebrate after spongers are ordered out of their home.* Accessed online: http://www.dailymail.co.uk/news/article-2034237/Victory-doctor-heavily-pregnant-wife-squatters-leave-home.html

*The Daily Mail.* 2011b. *Where my wife comes from, they SHOOT squatters: Doctor whose £1m home was taken over by spongers hits out at the law.* Accessed online: http://www.dailymail.co.uk/news/article-2035699/Squatters-shot-wife-comes-Doctor-1m-home-taken-spongers-hits-law.html

*The New York Times.* 2015. *Affordable housing, racial isolation.* Available online: http://mobile.nytimes.com/2015/06/29/opinion/affordable-housing-racial-isolation.html?smid=fb-share&_r=0&referrer

Timmins, N. 2001. *The Five Giants: A biography of the welfare state.* London: HarperCollins Publishers.

Touraine, A. 2000. *Can We Live Together? Equality and difference.* Cambridge: Polity Press.

Trust for London. 2021. *London households in temporary accommodation.* Accessed online: https://www.trustforlondon.org.uk/data/temporary-accommodation-borough/

Tudoroiu, T. 2014. Social media and revolutionary waves: The case of the Arab Spring, *New Political Science* 36(3): 346–365.

Tunstall, R. 2020. *The Fall and Rise of Social Housing: 100 years on 20 estates.* Bristol: Policy Press.

Turner, J. 2016. Governing the domestic space of the traveller in the UK: 'Family', 'home' and the struggle over Dale Farm, *Citizenship Studies* 20(2): 208–227.

Tyler, I. 2013. *Revolting Subjects: Social abjection and resistance in neoliberal Britain.* London, New York: Zed Books.

Tyler, I. 2020. *Stigma: The machinery of inequality.* London: Zed Books.

Tyler, I. and Slater, T. 2018. Rethinking the sociology of stigma, *The Sociological Review* 66(4): 721–743.

Unison. 2016. *Unison Briefing: The Housing and Planning Act 2016.* Accessed online: https://www.unison.org.uk/content/uploads/2016/08/Housing-and-Planning-Act-2016-FINAL.pdf

Urban, M. 2018. BrixtonBuzz. Accessed online: http://www.brixtonbuzz.com/2018/01/nobody-is-intentionallyhomeless-lobby-of-lambeth-council-meeting-weds-24th-jan/

Vasudevan, A. 2015. The makeshift city: Towards a global geography of squatting, *Progress in Human Geography* 39(3): 338–359.

Vasudevan, A. 2017. *The Autonomous City: A history of urban squatting.* London, New York: Verso.

Wacquant, L. 2007. Territorial stigmatization in the age of advanced marginality, *Thesis Eleven* 91(1): 66–77.

Waite, L. 2009. A place and space for a critical geography of precarity? *Geography Compass* 3(1): 412–433.

Walters, W. 2004. Secure borders, safe haven, domopolitics, *Citizenship Studies* 8(3): 237–260.

Watt, P. 2013. 'It's not for us': Regeneration, the 2012 Olympics and the gentrification of east London, *City* 17(1): 99–118.

Watt, P. 2016. A nomadic war machine in the metropolis: En/countering London's 21st century housing crisis with Focus E15, *City* 20(2): 297–320.

Watts, B. and Fitzpatrick, S. 2018. *Welfare Conditionality.* London: Routledge.

Weatherley, M. 2011a. *Early day motion 1545.* Accessed online: http://www.parliament.uk/edm/2010-12/1545

Webb, K. 2013. What's wrong with the bedroom tax? *Shelter briefing*. Accessed online: https://england.shelter.org.uk/__data/assets/pdf_file/0020/650 630/B edroom_tax_-_Shelter_briefing_March_2013.pdf

Weekes, T. 2018. Revealed – the true scale of affordable housing lost to permitted development rights. *Shelter blog*. Accessed online: https://blog. shelter.org.uk/2018/12/revealed-the-true-scale-of-affordable-housing-lost-to-permitted-development-rights/

Welshman, J. 2013. *Underclass: A history of the excluded since 1880*. London: Bloomsbury Academic.

Whitehead, C. 2021. The private rented sector – a crisis which will drag on and on? *Trust for London*. Accessed online: https://www.trustforlondon.org. uk/news/the-private-rented-sector-a-crisis-which-will-drag-on-and-on/

Wilcox, S. 2014. Housing benefit size criteria: Impacts for social tenants and options for reform. *Joseph Rowntree Foundation*. Accessed online: https:// www.jrf.org.uk/report/housing-benefit-size-criteria-impacts-social-sector-tenants-and-options-reform

Wilde, M. 2019. Resisting the rentier city: Grassroots housing activism and rentier subjectivity in post-crisis London, *Radical Housing Journal* 1(2): 63–80.

Wilkinson, E. 2013. Learning to love again: 'Broken families', citizenship, and the state promotion of coupledom, *Geoforum* 49: 206–213.

Wilkinson, E. and Ortega Alcázar, I. 2017. A home of one's own? Housing welfare for 'young adults' in times of austerity, *Critical Social Policy* 37(3): 329–347.

Williams, A. 2013. Squatters evicted from land where they were living despite having support of neighbours and judge saying they were 'not all bad'. *Mail Online*. Accessed online: http://www.dailymail.co.uk/news/article-2355511/Squatters-evicted-land-livingdespite-having-support-neighbours-judge-saying-bad.html?ito=feeds-newsxml

Wilson, W. 2016. Under-occupying social housing: Housing Benefit entitlement. *House of Commons Library Briefing Paper Number 06272*.

Wilson, W. and Barton, C. 2019. Private rented housing: The rent control debate. *House of Commons Library Briefing Paper Number 6760*.

Withnall, A. 2013. Squatters occupy Britain's most expensive council house on day it sells for £2.96 million. *The Independent*. Accessed online: http://www.independent.co.uk/news/uk/home-news/squatters-occupy-britain-s-most-expensive-council-house-on-day-it-sells-for-296m-8911319.html

# Index

intentional homelessness 66–67
permanence of 75–76
storage and removal costs 65
*see also* PLACE/Ladywell 'pop-up' social
housing scheme
territorial stigmatisation 24, 30
*see also* stigma
Thatcher, Margaret 8, 13, 27–29, 32, 37,
59, 79, 126
Touraine, Alain 105
tower blocks 40–41
Tower Hamlets 69
'troubled families' rhetoric 22–23, 32
Trump, Donald 105
Trust for London 12
Turner, Joe 18
Tyler, Imogen 23, 30

## U

'underclass' rhetoric 30, 31
unemployment, Cameron's political
rhetoric on 34
Universal Credit 128
housing element 43
University of York 60
Upper-tier Tribunals 103, 106
urban regeneration 12, 23, 31, 50
USA, housing policy 22

## V

van Lanen, Sander 121
Vasudevan, Alex 112–113

## W

Wacquant, Loïs 24
Walters, William 17–18, 35

war
as extreme domicide 5, 20, 21
and precarity 24
war veterans, Second World War 40, 80
warehouses, conversion to residential
accommodation 76, 77
Watt, Paul 23
Watts, Beth 26
Weatherley, Mike 84–85, 110, 125
welfare conditionality 32
welfare reform 32, 61, 121–122
Welfare Reform Act 2012 13, 43, 46, 54
*see also* bedroom tax (removal of the spare
room subsidy)
welfare sanctions 32
welfare state
development of 26, 39–40
and precarity 24–25
wellbeing
impact of bedroom tax on 52–54
impact of criminalisation of squatting
on 91–94
Whitten, Meredith 121
Wilde, Matt 109
Wilkinson, Eleanor 32, 61
women
and activism 117
sexism and misogyny in squatting 92–93
working class people 2, 4, 5, 9
and domicide 22–25
impact of the welfare state on 26
media representations of 31
stereotypes of 23

## Y

#YesDSS campaign 108–109

www.ingramcontent.com/pod-product-compliance
Lightning Source LLC
Chambersburg PA
CBHW070934030426

42336CB00014BA/2676